# *Big Sur Women*

*Edited by Judith Goodman*

*Designed by Pat Addleman*

*Big Sur Women Press, Box 40, Big Sur, Ca. 93920*

ISBN 0-9614678-0-0

Second printing, 1988

Cover photo by Joyce Rogers Lyke
Inset courtesy of Esther Ewoldsen

# Contents

# Foreword

*When, at the age of 42, I left my life as a Berkeley hills housewife and moved to Big Sur, I had no clear idea what I wanted to do with the rest of my life. I only knew that whatever it was, I wanted to do it here.*

*For three years I walked and I wandered alone in ever-widening circles from my cabin on the banks of the Big Sur River, coming to terms with the mess I had made of my life. In love with the land and immersed in myself, I had no need for social contact with the people who lived here.*

*I had not tasted solitude before. Now, a hunger that I'd never acknowledged could find satisfaction. As I discovered my natural bent—an aptitude, an appetite—for solitude and silence, my life slowly began to take on shape. By the end of three years I had found my work. After 20 fallow years, at last I was writing again, with a dedication intensified by decades of abstinence. Mornings in the meadow at my typewriter, afternoons in my garden or walking—my days flowed in a comforting rhythm. I found some sort of tentative balance without human contact.*

*Then Mother Nature, always the Prime Mover, staged one of the periodic shake-ups that punctuate our lives here in Big Sur. The Molera fire of 1972 followed by a winter of torrential rains and the great mud slides of '72-'73, forced me out of my self-imposed isolation. As always, in times of disaster, the community came together in fellowship. I began to meet people.*

*Mostly men at first. They were exceedingly visible—fighting the fire, repairing my waterline, bulldozing the wall of mud that threatened my cabin. They were rough and strong and indispensable. They told wonderful stories of legendary Big Sur men—men of superhuman strength and endurance. But where were the women? Did they manage to lead balanced lives on this isolated stretch of coast? In this seemingly man's world, did they find their place? I began to seek the women's stories.*

*The first woman whose life intrigued me was Grace Boronda. She too had come from Berkeley in middle age to make a new life for herself in Big Sur. What captured my romantic imagination was her surprise marriage to a Spanish cowboy and their pioneering life together. It sounded like my dream come true. With no clear goal in mind, I bought myself a tape recorder, drew up a list of people who had known Grace, and set off in search of her story.*

*Ten years later, as I sit down to weave Grace's story from the bits and pieces of her life that I have gathered, I realize that I know her more from within than from the stories that are told about her life. Then, as today, in Big Sur, where people live so separately and privately, the public image often bears little resemblance to the real person. It was only when I found my way into Grace's past and followed her to Berkeley to meet her niece who as a child had summered with the Borondas, that I caught a glimpse of the person. From this intimate glimpse, and by putting myself in Grace's place—walking the trails that she walked in her time, briefly living in her house, cooking in her kitchen, digging in her garden—by imagining myself as Grace, I have created a Grace Boronda who bears an uncanny resemblance to me.*

*The search has been fruitful. One woman has led to another. At first, quite at random, and then with increasing purpose, I have sought out women whose stories might be relevant to me in my quest for a perfect balance, and by extension, might inspire other women seeking to create authentic lives. The women in this collection, therefore, are a limited sample of Big Sur women. They have common concerns: how to cope with isolation from other women. I myself, my appetite for solitude quite satisfied, noted with envy that in the "outside world" women were finally coming together productively. I wanted some of that for myself and other Big Sur women.*

*With the aim of eventually publishing a periodical, I invited local women to join me in conducting interviews and gathering writings and graphics by and about Big Sur women. For four exhilarating months, twelve women worked together to launch the project, discovering in the course of meeting how hungry they had been for just such purposeful contact. We drew up a list of women we admired; interviews began. Then once again, Mother Nature intervened, bringing a series of monster storms to the coast, carrying Highway One, our lifeline, out to sea and effectively halting communication and travel. Not until April, 1984, 14 months later, was it possible to drive from one end of Big Sur to the other. Normal life ceased for the duration as we all concentrated on survival. BIG SUR WOMEN was shelved as a joint effort.*

*During these 14 months of enforced isolation, frustrating though they have been to my plans and ambitions, I have gained a deeper understanding of the joys and sorrows of a Big Sur woman's life. In this place I have chosen as home, where Nature still reigns supreme, I am learning to accept what I cannot change. I am learning surrender. In this lies the strength and the flexibility of Big Sur women.*

*I have chosen 18 stories of women who move me out of 120 years of Big Sur history. I can think of 50 other women who belong in this collection. But I feel a sense of urgency about its publication. My dear friend Harry Dick Ross, 85 years old, not only made me the gift of several of the choicest morsels in this book, but also has been my chief goad and inspiration. He wants to see this published in his lifetime. Elfrieda Hayes, whose memories of a pioneer childhood conjure up the early days, is 93; my new friend Virginia Swanson is 84. They can't wait forever. So, I am publishing this collection hoping that it may inspire other Big Sur women to join me in making this Volume One of a periodical.*

*If not, no matter. These women can stand alone.*

*Judith Goodman*
*Big Sur*

*At the age of forty-four, this Berkeley spinster fell in love -- first with the Big Sur coast, and then with a man of its people. Her life was never the same.*

# In Search of Grace Boronda

## by Judith Goodman

She stepped from the horse-drawn mail stage one day in early July, 1911, setting foot for the first time on the thick redwood duff before Pfeiffer's Resort in what is now Pfeiffer Big Sur State Park. She was tired from the all-day trip from Monterey in the simple wooden spring wagon, but excited by the fierce wild beauty of the coast. He'd been right, the professor who boarded in her mother's house on the edge of Berkeley's new campus. This was indeed a perfect place to vacation for an adventuresome woman who loved to walk.

Grace Elizabeth Biddle Roberts was a forty year old spinster when she first reached Big Sur. Born November 11, 1871, the fourth child of a spunky Irish immigrant and her mining engineer husband, Grace grew up in a family of five sisters and two brothers. The father's early death forced their mother to take in boarders in their large house close to the new campus of University of California. The girls did the chambermaid work and imbibed the heady intellectual atmosphere,

drawing their friendships from academic circles.

When Grace's brother Frederick struck it rich in African gold mines, he bought his mother a large home at the corner of Piedmont and Channing Way and declared that his mother would never work again.

From a niece, Sally Hawkins, who still resides in Berkeley, comes an intimate picture of Grace *en famille* -- constant squabbles among the unmarried sisters -- all strong, jealous, frustrated women, all eccentric. In the midst of this crowded household of eleven people, Grace lived in a third floor room seeking solitude. To her niece, Grace was the most interesting of the aunts -- Aunt Duck they called her -- with her flair for costumes, her guitar and her cello, with her flowers. To earn a living Grace grew flowers which she carried by ferry across the bay to San Francisco to sell to a fashionable florist. Branching out, she became a decorator for weddings and parties. This, and her love of concerts and plays, filled her life. She had a passion for the outdoors, roaming the unsettled hills behind Berkeley and Oakland, finding peace and solace from the hectic life among her brawling sisters. To live her own life was her greatest ambition.

Her first vacation at Pfeiffer's was a turning point for Grace. She fell in love with the coast. In a simple tent under the maples which she preferred to the tiny cabins renting for $3.00 a day including meals, this Berkeley woman discovered the exhilaration of independence. The resort run by Florence Pfeiffer took in a few guests each season. The guest register tells the story of early tourism in Big Sur -- a distinguished clientele -- the leading lights of Stanford and University of California, later artists and writers from Carmel: VanWyck Brooks, Lincoln Steffins, George Sterling, Jaime de Angulo, Robinson Jeffers, Ella Winters, Pete Steffins; and hunters and hikers, all adventuresome souls intent on exploring the unsettled wilderness that was then Big Sur. Among them, Grace Roberts arrived and her life was altered.

Grace is fondly remembered by the then six year old daughter of the Pfeiffers, Esther Ewoldsen, for after her first season, Grace became more than a paying guest, but "a friend of the family." If accommodations were crowded, Grace willingly gave up her tent and moved in with the girls. Esther recalls excursions with Grace to the swimming hole or down Sycamore Canyon to visit the Pfeiffer homestead as fascinating and illuminating adventures, for the woman was intensely alive and curious, and her enthusiasm was contagious. She was a vigorous walker, thinking nothing of donning her green corduroy divided skirt for an early morning walk across the flats of the Hill ranch to the lighthouse and back to the lodge before breakfast. As Esther remembers Grace, she was tall and in those days slender, radiating physical vitality. Dark, almost Spanish in appearance, her long dark hair was done up in a

"pouf." According to Florence Pfeiffer, "with her hair down her back in a braid and her nightgown on," Grace was beautiful.

Grace thrived on the simple healthy life of the Sur. It was a far cry from the steam-heated, overpopulated family home in Berkeley, and the "killing work," as she described her decorating job. For five seasons, in July, she returned for a month's vacation at the Pfeiffer Resort. She might have continued as an annual summer guest, dividing herself between the Sur and the city, had she not had the great good fortune to meet Alejandrino Boronda, the man on the well-behaved horse.

The resort functioned then as a post office and social center for the scattered pioneer families who inhabited the coast. There for his mail one day rode Boronda, one of the impoverished land grant Borondas who had once held vast ranch lands to the south. Now working as a ranch hand on the Hill ranch, he was a consummate horseman, in spite of a crippled leg from a childhood injury. Small and sparsely built, with a face like a proud eagle, he held himself straight with the pride of his ancestry. Grace took notice, discreetly, admiring his horse, Choppo, the only one of the local beasts, she said, which stood on all four legs while awaiting its master.

No one knew they were courting. The only person who might have been a party to the secret was Grace's good friend, Julia Pfeiffer, who is long dead. The Pfeiffer children, says Esther, were too young to notice such things. Perhaps the unlikely pair had caught each other's eyes on mail day, and then chanced to meet as Grace walked over the golden meadows to the lighthouse. Perhaps Grace had recognized her big chance in this silent rider on the palomino, and sought him out. She must have been a true romantic idealist and a woman of courage to leave the known world behind her, and set out on a new adventure at the age of forty-

10

four. It came as a complete surprise to the Big Sur community when on May 13, 1916, Grace Roberts became Grace Boronda. The wedding was witnessed by Maria and Amada Castro and was performed by a Catholic priest. Alejandrino was 35 at the time of his marriage. Grace gave her age as 34. She was actually ten years older.

There is a legend about their courtship which bears repeating, if only to link their story to the larger social scene on the coast. According to the story, Alejandrino sought the help of Jaime de Angulo, his riding companion and sometime employer, in his correspondence with Grace. Although his spoken English was excellent, his written language was imperfect, and Jaime was a learned man, a linguist. Jaime, as always a prankster, egged on by that legendary practical jokester "Roachie" Castro, wrote flowery, extravagant letters, making free with Alejandrino's dictation. It is rumored that the letters won her heart. When Grace learned of the practical joke after the wedding, the breach between the Borondas and the Castros and Jaime was immediate and long-lasting. The feud continued throughout their lives. As her niece Sally says, "Grace never forgot an insult. She loathed them."

The newly-weds began their life together at the Grimes homestead, a simple redwood cabin at the base of a steep barren slope, looking over Grimes Canyon to the sea. Very little remains now of the barn or cabin, but on the intact walls one can see Grace's touch -- over layers of the *Berkeley Gazette* used to keep the wind from blowing through the cracks, are the faded remains of the flocked wallpaper ordered from Montgomery Ward's. Always, no matter how primitive the conditions, Grace wanted things nice.

Life at the Grimes' homestead must have been difficult. The water supply was inadequate. The house stood surrounded by the arms of the mountain and above the fogline; the heat was intense. Still, they worked hard together, planted a gar-den, acquired a cow. But they dreamed of owning a piece of land. Here began the mutual passion that was to motivate their life -- the passion to possess land on the coast.

After a year at the Grimes' place, the couple found land to homestead on a rocky, steep and barren stretch of coast between Laffler and Torre Canyons. The work must have been killing to turn the inhospitable slope into a home, but fired by their strong commitment to their dream, and inspired by their growing devotion to each other, there emerged a pleasant house, a barn, outbuildings, an orchard, a garden. The first thing Grace did was plant maple trees to shade the house.

What an adjustment it must have been for Grace, used to a life of comfort and refinement. Supplies were brought in on horseback or mules. Heat was by woodstove. At first there was only an outdoor toilet. Of course, no electricity, no telephone, no highway. She adapted. Grace worked from dawn to dark, tending the garden, milking the cow, baking the bread, churning the butter, cooking on the new wood stove. Alejandrino raised cattle on their ever growing acres, hunted mountain lions for the $50.00 bounty with his dog Chongo, who treed over fifty lions in his time, and worked for other ranchers for cash. Any money the Borondas managed to accumulate was for buying more land. They were truly land poor. Over the forty years of their life in Big Sur, they accumulated 1400 acres of Big Sur land.

Working side by side with Alejandrino, wearing bib overalls in the fields, she was far from Berkeley. Yet, Grace did not totally abandon her past. Those who visited (and nobody came unexpectedly, for in addition to three separate gates before you reached the house, there were the guard geese and dogs to announce a visitor) would find Grace freshly attired in a cotton dress, prepared to offer whipped cream cake. Her library was extensive, especially her collection of California history. She read aloud to her husband in the evenings, played Caruso records on the wind-up victrola, collected baskets from Chinatown and rare teapots. Even in the wilderness, Grace liked things nice. Most emphatically, she looked down on the majority of Big Sur's rough and tough pioneer folk. The Borondas kept to themselves, rarely joining in the community's activities, living reclusive lives. The people of Big Sur considered them snobs.

The family in Berkeley were outraged by the marriage -- Grace had married a *farmer*. Perhaps the sisters were jealous -- no one of them ever married. Although visits from her siblings were few and far between, Grace's nieces became regular summer guests at Casa Boronda. From her niece Sally we get a picture of their life together -- hard work, much love, and a sweet regard for each other. Grace was very proper; there was "no running around without clothes on," even though the summers were hot. And when Aunt Duck took the girls to a community get-together at the Murphy ranch, they were forbidden to dance with "just anybody." When the Castros arrived, Grace insisted on their leaving the fandango because the drinking was going to get out of control. The nieces loved their summers with the Borondas, and adored Alejandrino, who told them stories and charmed them with his dark Spanish eyes.

They had very little social life. The nearest neighbors were the de Angulos, but he rode around naked on horseback and gave wild parties. She wanted nothing to do with him. Grace was choosy in her friendships -- Julia Pfeiffer Burns, the Overstroms, the Hathaways were among the select. Melodile Hathaway recalls one occasion when the Borondas and the Hathaways rode up to visit the Overstroms at Alta Vista, and another all-day ride to Burns Creek to see Julia Burns, followed by a bath at Slate's Hot Springs (now Esalen Institute), where one hung a white rag on a bush to warn others that the tubs were occupied. The Borondas made an

occasion of their ride to the post office, where on mail days the Big Sur community converged. Otherwise, they were reclusive.

I imagine that the twenty years before Highway One came through must have been blissful. Grace had everything she dreamed of -- a devoted husband whom she loved; an outdoor life full of good hard work, dogs, cats, chickens, geese, a cow, horses; a few good friends; books by mail courtesy of the County Library. True, she missed female companionship. True, she was alone a lot. True, their feuds with the neighbors escalated as they added parcels of land to their holdings. But all in all, those first twenty years were full and rich.

Then the road came through, the coast highway linking Monterey to the north with San Luis Obispo to the south, and Big Sur was opened to the world. The Borondas were among the few locals who bitterly opposed the change. Always fiercely protective of their privacy and of the sanctity of the land, they were threatened by the influx of convicts who worked on building the road. They began to keep a gun at the front door, and to tighten their security measures. Embittered by the change that they were helpless to prevent, Grace and Alejandrino watched with dismay as their carefully protected seclusion was invaded. They were never reconciled to the highway. Certainly, it was now easier to drive to Monterey for the day and browse the antique stores with her friend Melodile Hathaway. Certainly, it was now much simpler to get supplies. But she resented the tourists who littered, and the vandals who desecrated the land she held sacred. From the opening of the road in 1937, Grace's life began to darken.

A series of misfortunes punctuates the last decade of her life. A soldier from Fort Ord somehow surprised Grace alone and attempted rape. Grace's hip was broken. Taken to Oakland for surgery, she spent months recovering. Determined to return to the ranch, she did so, although the hip did not heal right; from then on she was lame. It must have been very hard to drag herself up the steep flight of stairs to the Boronda bedroom, and to manage the uneven terrain of that rocky piece of land.

Sometime in the winter of 1954, in the midst of one of Big Sur's savage southwest storms, Grace, alone at the time, attempted to shut the heavy barn door. It was caught by the wind, Grace was swept off her feet, her arm pulled from the socket, her hip injured. When Alejandrino returned, he found her in a state of shock. Taken to a Monterey hospital, she never recovered and died on May 26, 1954.

Alejandrino Boronda lived for nine more years, but he too never recovered from the shock of her death, and the last of his life was spent briefly at Agnews State Hospital and later in the care of Ray Jones, one of his former employees. The property was bought by Melodile Hathaway, who has kept it intact to this day.

The last chapter of her story is sad, ending in ashes and dust. But as niece Sally Hawkins reminds me, we must concentrate on what she had -- the fulfillment of her dreams and many years of active life on her beloved land. I am certain that Grace would not have had it any other way.

*Courtesy of Sally Hawkins*

*Last Portrait: Grace and Alejandrino Boronda*

*An idyllic childhood at the turn of the century was not without moments of sadness for Elfrieda Hayes. "This old coast," sighed the young Elfrieda. "I wished we lived in town. Here a person has money and nowhere to spend it."*

# A Pioneer Girlhood on the North Sur Coast: Elfrieda Swetnam Hayes

## by Deborah Johansen

*In those days, we had Carmel, Doud's and Soberanes' Creek, Souza's place, Garapatos and Abalone Bay. In those days, Big Sur was a far away country.*

Just as the land was not then known as one broad sweep of Big Sur country, but was checkered into family holdings -- deep canyons and winding creeks bearing the names of the first settlers -- so the young life of Elfrieda Inez Swetnam took on a fabric as colorfully patterned as the lay of the land. The canyon characters, the outlandish pranks she and her playmates would pull on each other, daily treks to the school at Bixby, dances at Notley's Landing, and even the more pensive or complaining times -- all were woven into the memorable pioneer childhood of the only surviving member of the Swetnam family.

Born in Garrapata Canyon on March 29, 1891 to Isaac Newton and Ellen Jane Swetnam, Elfrieda was the youngest of nine children. Both former schoolteachers from Kentucky, the Swetnams made their way west as far as Wichita, Kansas where they enjoyed relative prosperity from Mr. Swetnam's thriving restaurant and store business. A case of malaria which Mrs. Swetnam and her baby Mary contracted

forced them to head west on doctor's orders once again in 1882. As Ellen Swetnam reported at the time, however, with her usual dry wit, "Newt always had itchy feet, and I was glad when we got to the Pacific Ocean because he couldn't go anywhere unless he swam." "And he was a good swimmer," adds Elfrieda today.

After an abrupt introduction to country living in Felton -- raising strawberries and chopping wood for a living -- the Swetnams heard of cheap timber claims to the south, and in 1887, Mr. Swetnam moved bags, baggage and his brood of wife and seven children down the coast and inland to the north fork of the Little Sur River, under the sheer slopes and massive redwoods of Pico Blanco. The feather bed was roped onto the back of a mule on top of which perched, precariously, baby Mary. Everyone else tramped along behind to the new homestead.

In 1889, with seven children nearing school age, the Swetnams moved once again back over the mountain to the coast, building a small, two-story house in Garrapata Canyon. Life was far less harsh, and the road and neighbors more accessible than at Pico Blanco. But the Swetnams still had a lot to learn about life on the coast. Only through the timely intervention of their new neighbor, Mr. Souza, did Isaac Swetnam escape the wrath of a lynching party, old Mr. Souza patiently explaining to the local vigilantes that young Mr. Swetnam's attempt to clear his land by fire had accidentally flared out of control and that he was not purposely trying to burn out his neighbors in the canyon.

It was here in Garrapata Canyon on March 29, 1891 that Elfrieda Inez Swetnam was born -- the last of nine children -- delivered by local midwife, Mrs. Alpress, and bathed and dressed by her older sister Florence (later Florence Swetnam Pfeiffer, mother of Mrs. Esther Ewoldsen of Big Sur). It was not long before Elfrieda displayed a certain independence. She was precocious, had a gentle sense of humor, a quick wit, a weakness for mischief and a love of her natural surroundings on the coast. She had red hair, expressive eyes and a sensitivity that endeared her to many.

Her father was honest, tremendously hardworking and "never profane." A former teacher and businessman-turned-pioneer-farmer, "he made a good living for us -- the best butter, honey and cheese," which he would take to Monterey to sell. He had a penchant for whist, cribbage and cards which he taught Elfrieda -- but he would never gamble out of respect for Mrs. Swetnam. He could be a stern disciplinarian, but was usually gentle and soft-spoken. Mrs. Swetnam was a large woman, with a chronically weak constitution, whose round face was framed by dark, crimped curls. She was proud of her intellect and schooling, boasted a voluminous library, and an astonishing memory for all she read. She carefully recorded events of the day in a small journal written with "a hand like a copyplate". She encouraged the children, especially Elfrieda, to read and often lost her patience with their endless questions, "telling us to look it up in the encyclopedia and not bother her in the kitchen."

Elfrieda and her older brother, Manoah Newton, were both loyal compatriots in mischief around house and farm. Although only three years older, Manoah managed to think up enough trouble for both himself and his baby sister, and Elfrieda was always the willing partner-in-crime. One summer afternoon he convinced Elfrieda to test the Swetnam stock of vintage mead, asking her to pass on any that seemed particularly tasty -- and to keep tasting until she found something palatable. Not long thereafter, the Swetnams returned from strawberrying to find a very tipsy little girl and her equally red-faced brother. Occasional raids on the cucumber and cantaloupe patches for snacks were not uncommon much to their mother's despair.

Animals were a source of delight to Elfrieda. She was especially fond of cats and had a "common black and white cat named Tommy" as a pet. She also kept a pet rabbit (a near victim to the cat) and a somewhat more exotic pair brought by a boarder who had been sojourning in South America: a monkey, and a parrot by the name of Corinta who would sing endless refrains of "After the Ball" in Spanish and curse the cattle-drivers in a blue streak of Spanish from the upper reaches of the "gum" (eucalyptus) trees.

However young, Elfrieda still had the importance of small chores -- grinding the coffee beans which Mrs. Swetnam prided herself in roasting before each meal, and feeding the chickens. She and Manoah would also be routinely dispatched to the vegetable garden to trap gophers. At five cents a gopher, she saved enough pocket money until the Fourth of July to buy firecrackers, and from then on until Christmas for presents. As the youngest of the family she escaped most chores, and the brunt of the work went to her parents, older sisters and brothers and to the hired hands, leaving Elfrieda free to her own thoughts and adventures.

Her greatest loves and private haunts were the beaches below Garrapata and Palo Colorado Canyons:

*I lived on the beach! I'd hunt for arrowheads and other Indian artifacts, beautiful shells, explore the caves or just idle the hours, sunning on the sand. I don't know why they let me roam around, but they must have felt that I'd be all right, because I would go down to the beach for hours. We had seven beaches then, one sand beach and the rest were rocky. Just below the southern end of the beach -- about a mile from the mouth of Garrapata -- was beautiful Abalone Bay, just full of abalone. One day I'd been messing around those tide pools, not paying any attention to where I was going, and here was a big sea lion. Oh, was I ever scared! He was taking a sunbath, and I almost had my hand on him, and he was just as scared as I was. He went over into the deeper water right then. I don't know how they ever trusted me to be wandering down on the beach, but they did. I just loved the water.*

In 1896 (Elfrieda was five), the Swetnams bought a sizeable piece of land in the next canyon that ran from Rocky Point to Souza's place. Hewing all the logs before his carpenter arrived from Pacific Grove, Isaac Swetnam soon built a three-story frame house that was a specimen of construction for the times on the coast. Part brick and mortar, part hewn logs and shingled, it nestled in a sun-swept pasture at the mouth of Palo Colorado Canyon, bordered on the north by high eucalyptus trees. (The house is still found on the original site and is now owned by Electa Grimes' family.) By the end of 1896, the Swetnam family moved into their new house. The amenities were simple but sufficient: no indoor toilet, but the bathroom boasted a tub and running water piped down from the flume up the creek. "The outhouse at least had the dignity of a Montgomery Ward catalog rather than the usual corn cob."

Neighbors included Mr. Souza, in whom Elfrieda took a great deal of interest, for his planting of cypress were exactly her age. Below Notley's Landing on land now known as Westmere, lived Dick Smith and his large family of daughters. "Old man Smith said beans were the staff of life, and I never ate there that they didn't have beans and the best home made bread. Rocky Creek was considered their territory and Palo Colorado ours."

Between the two families, there was a mutual respect for property and its wealth of abalone, mussels and wild berries -- hospitality was almost limitless and bounty of land given upon asking. Others in the canyon at the time included the Sterrets, Vandalls, (people said Mr. Vandall was crazy but that was because he believed in spiritualism and said if anyone cut his trees after he died he would come back to haunt them) Murrays, Sauls and Old-Man Vogler: "a one-armed man who lived way back in the hills, who was also so good to all us kids." One day, to the squeals of delight and open-mouthed wonder of Elfrieda and her friends who had never seen snow, Mr. Vogler hefted down from the mountains a huge bucket of the stuff, cold and white and wonderful!

As the youngest, Elfrieda's life seemed to move with the seasons -- idling on the sand, berrying in the open fields, and generally being a tomboy -- to the despair of her mother's refined sensibilities. On at least one day, Elfrieda ran indoors breathlessly with a great tear in her skirt. "Friedie, Friedie," sighed Mrs. Swetnam, "how am I ever going to mend that?" To which Elfrieda piped up brightly, "Oh, you can just (ma)'chine it up in a minute!"

It was probably due to Elfrieda's rough-housing with the boys that Mrs. Swetnam decided Elfrieda needed some learning in the more womanly arts. So her sisters set about teaching Friedie to cook -- "beginning with the nice things so she'll always love to cook," which has proven true to this day. Her favorites were large batches of Sand Tart cookies baked up from Cleveland's Baking Powder book. But domestic duties were primarily relegated to the kitchen, for "my sisters said they wouldn't teach me to milk, because then I would never have to do it as a chore."

Elfrieda's childhood was not without moments of sadness or loneliness due to the isolation of the coast and the rough life it sometimes held for a little one. On an especially dreary winter day, Mrs. Swetnam found her youngest staring soulfully out the window into the pouring rain.

"This old coast," she sighed. "I wished we lived in town. Here a person has money and nowhere to spend it."

"Well, Friedie, how much do you have?" her mother asked softly.

And rising to her small height, Friedie announced indignantly, "I got fifteen cents!"

All too soon Elfrieda was eight and old enough to make the daily three-mile trip with Manoah and her sisters to the one-room schoolhouse at Bixby Creek, then called Mill Creek. Sometimes the children would walk, picking up neighbor children along the way -- more often they would ride horseback or be driven in the horse drawn "buckboard" cart. (The schoolhouse was destroyed in the flood of 1908.) Almost the youngest, Elfrieda began at one of the smaller desks up front as Mrs. Florence Hogue, school-mistress-cum-postmistress, presided over a motley group of nineteen youngsters comprising first through ninth grades. Elfrieda had an insatiable appetite for reading which academically placed her well above the other children her age. "My mother had a great many books, and I can remember sneaking up to the third floor and reading them -- books that were way beyond me, but reading them just the same." Her intellectual curiousity, however, never managed to spill over into arithmetic which remained her *bete noir* until she mastered her multiplication tables in the seventh grade. Not only did school introduce a daily routine to her life, it also meant the end of barefeet and carefree puttering on the Rocky Creek beach and around the farm. It was Elfrieda's introduction to black stockings and high buttoned shoes -- *de rigeur* for young ladies even on the south coast.

*Our feet were so tough we could light a match on the bottom of our feet and not feel it! For my first shoes, my father put my feet on a piece of paper and drew a line around it and rode the many miles to town to buy my first pair. But they were laced so tight that when I got up to recite, I fainted from the pain and had to be carried down to the creek where I could take off my shoes and soak my feet.*

The throng of school children included the Brazil boys, Smith girls, Swetnams, Souzas, Soberanes and even a Chinese boy, Wing, who intrigued the other children with his long queue and stories of China. He was a sensitive child whom Elfrieda befriended when he was made fun of by his playmates. They were mischievous group if left to their own devices -- Elfrieda no less than the others.

As the summer stretched leisurely between school seasons, the schoolhouse itself took on a more festive atmosphere -- dances, Fourth-of-July parties, mussel bakes and barbeques.

Summers for Elfrieda not only meant freedom from lessons and high buttoned shoes, but treasured weeks with her best girlfriend Myrtle Allen, who came from San Francisco to visit her Aunt Martha Bixby on the coast.

Other summer days she spent with the rowdy group of six to eight boys boarding with the Swetnams each summer at what was probably the first boys' ranch on the coast. She would hold her own at target practice with the 22 rifle, joining them to fish in the creeks or clamber over the rocks above the beach.

"Although we were never sweethearts," Elfrieda took an instant liking to one of the boys, young Jim Heyneman visiting from Belvedere. They were inseparable pals -- he often defending her honor when boys got fresh -- and continued the pranks she had played many years earlier with Manoah.

*One time when we were a little older, we were out walking around the drive, and some people offered us a ride. We couldn't very well refuse it, and when they asked, Jim told them we were just married and on our honeymoon. (We told them these wild lies!) And at any rate, they said, "Well, where are you staying?" And we said, "Hotel Del Monte." Well, we put our foot in it that time, because they insisted on taking us back to the hotel, and then we had to walk all the way back!*

But there were also quiet times to become closer to the softer feeling of the coast and to know and love it as a special place to live.

*On nice evenings we would walk from the house on the road to where this hill rose and watch the Point Sur light flash -- first red and then white. Nowadays that would seem a very tame pastime, but it was a pleasant walk in those days, and the young folks especially liked it. Oh, sometimes I felt abused to be living in the country, but most of the time, I sure loved that place. No girl ever had a nicer place to live and grow up. It was a privilege to live there then.*

It is particularly fitting that the family name of Swetnam, carried down from its old English forebear, "Sweatingham," means "sweet home."

*Sources: This oral history was compiled in part from taped interviews with Elfrieda Hayes by the author and by Beverly Newell and Penny Vieregge, and from an interview with Esther Ewoldsen by Judith Goodman, and from letters and written testimony from Elfrieda Hayes.*

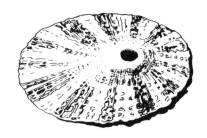

Photo by Pat Addleman

# Two Pioneer Sisters

## by Esther Ewoldsen

*Since first I chanced upon Mary Ellen's lovely, lonely grave on NoName Ridge, standing within its own small picket fence separate from two other Pfeiffer gravestones, the thought of her has haunted me. Who was this woman who lies under a blanket of Naked Ladies on a grassy knoll above the blue Pacific? Why did she die a young woman?*

*There is no one alive today in Big Sur who knew Mary Ellen. There is only "hearsay" evidence, not admissible in court. Still, the source of this hearsay is Mary Ellen's niece, Esther Pfeiffer Ewoldsen, a wise Big Sur woman of great sympathy, who tells the little she knows. Enough to reveal the bare bones of a tragic life.*

*Judith Goodman*

She was a little over three years old when the family came to Big Sur in 1869. She must have been expected to help in the family at an early age, being the oldest girl. At age twenty-two she bore an illegitimate child. She never did name the father of the child nor whether he was transient or neighbor. The Pfeiffer genes were so strong that the child was "Pfeiffer" with no other telltale features. The general attitude in those days was very censorious of the girl who bore a child out of wedlock. Undoubtedly, Mary Ellen's life was very unhappy.

She married Alvin Dani probably about 1895. I have no exact date. It was sometimes said that Alvin was more attracted to Mary Ellen's sister Kate but that Mary Ellen had more money. (Where did the money come from? The children were given a heifer calf at an early age and that was the nucleus of a herd in later years with luck and good management.)

*Mary Ellen Pfeiffer Dani*
*July 14, 1866 -- Sept. 24, 1900*

The Danis lived at first at the old Anderson Place (Burns Creek) where the house was on a bench with a small stream running near the door. Mary Ellen had some trout that she planted in this little stream, with flowers and vegetables nearby. Later, they lived on Pico Blanco. Did Alvin homestead there? Did he rent the land or buy? The area is still named Dani Ridge.

It was there that Mary Ellen died. The third child by Alvin was well on the way and Alvin was getting ready to go on a trip somewhere. Mary Ellen, feeling that he would be seeing Kate while gone, told him that if he left her, she would take her life. Either he did not believe her or he didn't care for he continued his preparations for going, saddling his horses at the barn. Mary Ellen took strychnine, and though the illegitimate child, then eleven, ran to the barn saying, "Mama is awfully sick," it was too late. She left one daughter aged three and another aged one, beside the eleven year old.

I did not know this aunt of mine who died before I was born, but since she was a Pfeiffer, I do know that she was a good worker.

*In contrast, here is Julia, Mary Ellen's younger sister, whose life was full of joy and satisfaction. What is the secret ingredient that makes one life a tragedy and the other a triumph?*

*Julia Pfeiffer Burns*
*Nov. 20, 1868 -- Jan. 25, 1928*

Julia was less than a year old in 1869 when Michael and Barbara Pfeiffer made their hazardous journey down the wild uninhabited Sur coast to become Big Sur's first permanent settlers. While the parents and the older son Charles cleared the land all day to plant the first crop, tiny seven year old brother John cared for the babies, Julia and Mary Ellen, three, and cooked the beans for the mid-day meal. The baby was heavy and hard to manage, until John discovered that when tripped, Julia could be rolled around and changed as necessary.

As pioneer children must, Julia learned early the many skills needed to be self-sufficient. More interested in caring for the farm animals than in housework, nevertheless, Julia had to learn all household duties as well as sewing, knitting, embroidery, and Spanish drawn-work. Reminiscing with her niece, Esther Pfeiffer Ewoldsen, she remembered never having a new pair of stockings, since as soon as she finished knitting one she would have to put it on, thus always wearing one new and one well-worn.

The Pfeiffer family grew and prospered, the boys took up claims of their own along the coast (at one time, it is said, there was a Pfeiffer on every ridge). The girls married, all except Julia, who took over more and more of the ranch chores as her father aged, until it was she who ran the ranch. She cared for the stock, plowed, planted and mowed the hay, milked the cows, kept the machinery in repair, helped with the flower and vegetable gardens, while Barbara ruled the roost. It was said that when Barbara spoke to her husband, one looked around to see who was the ten year old boy she addressed.

As customary for a spinster daughter Julia remained at home, a "dependent," until well into middle age. She made an attempt to prove up a parcel of land above the dunes at Pfeiffer Beach, building a cabin; one weathered corner post still stands, and a patch of Naked Ladies, which follow the Pfeiffers wherever they go. Although she never completed the process of acquiring title, she must have enjoyed the cabin as a retreat from her busy and family-circumscribed life.

Hard work was her life. That, and the stretch of empty beach at the foot of the canyon, and the lilac-covered hills above the ranch. As soon as the danger of grizzly bears had been eliminated (by hanging strychnine-larded meat from a tree, out of reach of the dogs), Julia was safe to wander and explore. When the endless farm chores were over, she found moments to enjoy her favorite beach. In later years, she led her nieces and nephews on many joyous excursions to what now is "Pfeiffer Beach." Julia loved people, picnics, dances and whipped cream cakes. She loved life.

Not until well past middle age, in about 1915, did Julia marry John Burns, an early homesteader, and move south down the coast, where the newly-weds lived at the Anderson Place (Burns Creek). They ran cattle on leased pasture at Saddle Rock Ranch. Julia and John lived and worked together in great contentment. Together they shared the inside and outside chores and cared for the cattle, she riding pell-mell up and down the hills, he slowly making his way on foot or riding more slowly. Later they rented the Hot Springs (now Esalen Institute), and Julia provided meals and accommodations for visitors to the hot springs. She worked hard and enjoyed life.

Women friends were few and far between. Although the differences in background were great between them, she formed close friendships with three city transplants to Big Sur, Grace Boronda from Berkeley, Beth Livermore of a prominent East Bay family, and Helen Hooper Brown of Boston, whose husband, Lathrop Brown, had been a Harvard roommate of FDR. when the Browns were in residence at their Saddle Rock Ranch, Julia became Mrs. Brown's close friend and mentor, teaching from her vast store of practical frontier knowledge.

In later life, when the work became too arduous, the couple bought a small piece of land near Salinas, where they lived a quiet life without extremes of toil. Here, an old abdominal complaint required hospitalization, and she died in 1928, probably of cancer.

When the Saddle Rock Ranch property was gifted to the state of California, Mrs. Brown chose to name the State Park in honor of this capable pioneer woman. Julia Pfeiffer Burns State Park is a monument to a hard and happy life.

*

*A woman whose girlhood was spent on Partington Ridge remembers her summertime joys.*

# The Road to Kate's

## by Heidi Hopkins

It is evening, one of those long summer evenings promising whole worlds to explore between dinner and bedtime. The gate's spring chatters rustily as I slip through and skip down the two steps to the road. Dinner is over; I'm off to Kate's.

My feet skate along the worn surface of the road. I feel the solid pressure of the ground, the familiar ruts and contours. Oaks, madrones and pines form a tunnel through which I descend. Pine scent wafts in the air; dust billows up from my feet as I scuff the road; towhees buzz and scratch in the undergrowth, speckled by the sun's amber rays. Towards the end of the tunnel I break into a leaping run and burst out to the wide grassy world that rolls steeply down to Kate's. Here, as always, I cut off from the road. I examine the dams and canals and irrigation systems we built from mud and hollow grass blades in the spot underneath the madrone where the water line leaks. A gopher has destroyed one canal and two fields. I walk out on the point and crouch on the brink to survey.

The fog, heaving in the slanting rays of sun, hugs the knees of the coast. It blankets the ocean, the highway; isolates our hills. The trees behind cut off my house. The sky arches over my head to meet the crest of the ridge where sentinel pines stand guard. I am alone in the aerie. The air is sweet, warm and cricket-pulsing.

The fog spread out at my feet is a world of shadowed canyons and steep-sided hills where everyone would be weightless, where running up the sides of hills and bounding from rise to rise would be effortless. A world tantalizingly within reach of my eyes yet just beyond the reach of my legs. If I could only jump out far enough...one huge leap would carry me to that cloudy world. It is too far. My eyes rove so much farther than my legs. Along the coast the ridges glow in the amber light. Spotted here and there yuccas send up plumes of white like candle flames along the flanks. Patches of meadow between the chamise and the woods play games with my imagination: on the near ridge is a cave inhabited by a troll (I can see him perched above the entrance), across the canyon a wild horse rears. Birdsong cascades down the steep canyons to meet the rising sigh of the streams. Jumping up, I add my shout to theirs out over the expanse. The call floats back out of the canyon in a wavering echo. I play with the echo, shouting it down, encouraging it along. Hello! Hello!

I run back to the road with my shoes stuffed with stickers. I bound down the steep, gravelly section of road to where my path to Kate's diverges from the road which winds along the forest's edge. Here, I take off through the fields to the first of the rolling staircase of hills that drop off to Kate's. At the top of the first rise I stop and peer down to the large madrone that hides Kate's house on the edge of the woods. Kate is waiting for me on the crest of her hill. We call to each other with big hellos that echo out of the canyon in a tangle of sound. We wave our arms big and wide over our heads. Hello! And down I run through the fields, soft and gopher-pocked. The summer grasses, stiff, dried, pods splayed, tickle my legs. I cut a path of silence through the cricket song as I go.

I duck under the barbed-wire fence that crosses the field at its lower end and regain the road. Kate is halfway down the steep path that leads from her house to the Crossroads where the road to her house joins the road to mine. The Crossroads marks the edge of Kate's world as the tunnel of trees marks the edge of mine. The fields in between are shared. Spring arrives first at the Crossroads with the blooming of the johnny-jump-ups, their yellow pansy faces beaming up through the February storms and the south winds. Kate always spots the first one and announces spring. Now the Crossroads is deep in dust. Kate is barefoot, as always. I take off my shoes and we send up puffs of dust between our toes.

We walk back to the fields, Kate and I, back under the barbed-wire fence to our sunset overlook. As the last spark of sun winks out between the contours of the fog, we breathe a ritual "good night." When the horizon has deepened to a pale green we get up to go; I trudge up the hill and Kate takes the path to her house. We turn and call to each other as we go. We have our special calls. They echo familiarly in the canyon until we are each just a speck in the dusk. Then I turn and charge up the steep hill to the trees.

I reenter the oak tunnel at the top of the fields. Inside it is dark but no less familiar to me for that. The shadowy outline of things guides my way: dark stripes of roots and ruts, the heavy trunks of trees, now on this side, now on that. I know the crevices, the bends, the contours of this world, the last stretch of road to home. I reach our gate in darkness. It chatters welcome and bangs behind me. The fog has risen some, pale in the night, pulled up tight against the shoulders of the coast. I leave my sticker-filled shoes outside the house. It's time for bed. Tomorrow I will adventure again.

*A young school teacher writes of her journey in 1891 over the Santa Lucias to the Big Sur coast, and of the small community she serves as teacher.*

# Over the Santa Lucia

## by Mary L. White

*Reprinted from THE OVERLAND MONTHLY, November, 1892.*

### I

In a hollow on the seaward side of the Santa Lucia mountains, about sixty miles south of old Monterey, is such a community as one reads about, but seldom sees. . . .

It was in August, 1891, that I bade farewell to civilization, and set my face southwestward, with this place as an objective point. About noon we entered Monterey County. Fremont's Peak loomed in sight on the left, and the names of the stations, such as Pajaro (Pa-ha-ro) and Soledad, reminded the passenger that he was on ground that had belonged to an earlier civilization than ours.

As we came further south it grew hotter, and dryer, and dustier, and flatter. Trees became scarcer, and the few that remained to illustrate the survival of the fittest had set their branches southward as if fleeing before the wind. Great wheatfields spread out to right and left. The blue line of the Gabilan Mountains on the left, and a straggling line of gray willows skirting some small stream on the right, gave a needed relief of color to the glaring yellow of the stubble.

The passengers became fewer, and those who boarded the train were of a different type. The heat was intense, and the portly Spanish don took off his wide straw hat, and mopped and fanned with plebian vigor. . . .

About half-past two P.M. we reached Kings City, a dry and dusty but thriving town. Here we left the train for the stage. . . .Imagine, a little, old, dried-up, two-seated, shabbily-covered vehicle, drawn by two horses that looked as though they would stand without holding until they died from inanition, and you will be near the facts.

After driving westward for ten more flat, hot, and dusty miles we began to ascend a mountain, in the shadow of which it grew much cooler. This was a comparatively insignificant outlying guard of the Santa Lucia Range, covered with scrub liveoak and chamisal brush.

After four o'clock we encountered many dirty-faced urchins with bare and dusty feet and gleaming tin pails, "just let loose from school," and occasionally, we had a view of the homely and sometimes squalid interior of some redwood shanty,

with the mother and a half-a-dozen small children sitting about the porchless door.

After coming down the opposite side of the mountain we drove through groves of large white oaks, with graceful, drooping branches.

It was twilight as we neared the little sleepy hollow town of Jolon (Ho-lone). From thence the journey was to be on horseback, baggage being carried on mules. There is no regular means of conveyance at all, and even no mail-service beyond this point, except a bi-weekly mail by carrier to the Los Burros mines and Pacific Valley, thirty miles to the south-westward on the coast.

Through a mistake in dates I was obliged to wait here three days. One would scarcely remain from choice, at this season of the year, as Jolon enjoys the reputation of being the hottest place above ground.

The civilization, however, is of some interest as a study. English, Americans, Danes, Spanish and Mexicans are scattered around. Ordinary social distinctions are dropped, and your vis-a-vis at table may be anyone, from a blacksmith or stage-driver to a retired army officer in the person of

"mine host", or a Church of England clergyman, of which denomination there was a representative during my stay. If the days are disagreeable, the evenings almost compensate, and only fail to do so on account of their brevity. They are balmy as the tropics; the katydids made music, and we sat on the veranda in long stretches of easy silence, broken occasionally by the jog-trot gait and jingling spurs of some passing horseman. Occasionally one stopped and asked for mail, or for tobacco, for our hotel is store and postoffice also. Two or three Spanish youths loitered on the steps, talking in soft, broken English, or in their own more musical language. Our clergyman drifted, as it were, from his seat further back, until he was among them, and though he had probably not met one of them before, they mixed without a ripple, and the talk glided on, or paused, with equal unconstraint, as though they were friends of everyday. One wondered if it was the touch of religion and humanity, or the effect of the climate.

When the stage rattled in, even this sound was subdued in keeping with the scene. There was no hurry, no loud or quick tones, as it unloaded its one or two passengers and its few mailbags. Even these failed to create any excitement. . . .

One evening at dusk -- one scarcely troubles himself to count in such a place -- a horseman jingled in, leading a saddled horse, and followed by a small black mule. He was "Baptiste," I was told, who had come to take me over the mountains on the following day. I shook hands with a dark, crippled, middle-aged little Spaniard, rather intelligent and kindly looking, but not speaking much *Ingles*, as he told me.

Next morning we rose betimes, intending to start at six; but it was half-past six when my baggage wa strapped on the mule, and we were ready to mount. Probably never in his existence had that mule known the honor of carrying fifty pounds of Shakespearean and philosophical literature, with the English poets thrown in; but he seemed not to appreciate it, for he eyed the box suspiciously, and showed a disposition to kick when the blind was removed.

By unusual good fortune a driver of a buckboard happened to be going our route, and for a consideration was induced to take me to the foot of the mountain; that is, as far as it is possible to go in any kind of conveyance. My driver, like my mounted escort, was Spanish, or Spanish-Mexican, and spoke even less English than the latter. He was of a different type, however, being stern and stubborn looking, while he of the horse was smiling and meek, and apparently childlike, though one now and then suspected a latent spiritual kinship to Bret Harte's heathen Chinee.

We had gone ten miles westward, when we came upon the ruins of the old San Antonio Mission, founded one hundred and fifteen years ago, and one of the most picturesque missions in California. It stands on a large plain, skirted on three sides by mountains. Six thousand Indians once belonged to this mission, and the remains of their adobe dwellings dot the plain in every direction. A few gnarled apple and pear trees have survived the general decay, and seem almost animate with their weight of memories. . . .

No thought seems to be taken to prevent the old mission from falling to pieces, a neglect one can scarcely regret when he contemplates the irredeemable badness of some "restored" California missions. Occasionally an artist with an eye for effective ruins happens along, and paints these old sanctuaries. Many daubers put them on shells and bits of wood, and furnish the bazaar stores of California watering places with "souvenirs of California," to sell to the gullible Eastern tourists for fifty cents. But the average Californian is a creature of the present. He looks forward, and not back; he has no time for reminiscence, and is in general a stranger to the sentiment of reverence for the old and traditional.

An hour before noon we drove up to an adobe house, the home of "Hidalgo," the driver. Evidently he was a bachelor, for there was no sign of women or children. A tall, Apache-like Indian appeared, and cooked tortillas, and made coffee, which with melons formed the meal of the host. I had brought my lunch, and while I ate this, and shared the melons, Baptiste changed the horses.

I said there was no evidence of the presence of women, and I believe the Spanish master and the Indian cook were the sole occupants of the house. But a bucket of half-starved flowers hung from the edge of the porch, in its dry and desolate surroundings and rough human environment not without its suggestion of pathos. There were cats and dogs galore; probably kept to compensate for the lack of human society.

We drove five miles farther, though there was not the least evidence of a road. Another house marked the point where horseback travel became a necessity, but this one was built of redwood "shakes," and its entire surroundings seemed thriving and progressive. Its owner came up on horseback, -- a young man, half American and half German, and wholly modern and alert. There immediately ensued between him and my driver a lively quarrel as to the ownership of the land and house. The former had the good nature of secure possession, and flourished in his opponent's face the proof in the shape of a legal document. He appealed to me as the only competent and disinterested party present to read the proof of his homestead. With the help of free translation by himself and Baptiste, Hidalgo was probably more convinced than was pleasant, for he mounted his buckboard and drove off in high dudgeon, threatening diverse sorts of summary vengeance.

We had ridden five miles under a burning sun when another adobe appeared. It was the home of Baptiste's mother, and the last house on this side of the mountains. We were glad to dismount and rest under the old vine-covered porch, while the mother cooked the dinner, and one of Baptiste's boys drove up fresh horses from the pasture. As these appeared on the gallop Baptiste stood ready, there was a *whir*, and one of the animals stood still, having learned from experience not to struggle against the riata.

The conservatism of these Spanish families is remarkable. Here was this house built of adobe, just as the old California homes of one hundred years ago were built. The old Mission grapevines knotted and coiled themselves over the porch. Chickens and little pigs shared the shade with Baptiste's children, just as other chickens and little pigs had shared the shade of other adobes with the *muchachitos* of a century ago. Here was a grown-up brother of Baptiste's, probably twenty-five years old, who spoke no English, not having been allowed to go the school for fear of contracting American habits, and being led away from the religion of his fathers.

When the dinner came there were tortillas, and rice, and beans. If the ghost of Baptiste's great-great- grandfather could have appeared, he would probably have forgotten the airy nothingness of his present constitution, and have fallen to with a natural appetite.

When we mounted again, it was to begin the actual ascent of the higher ridges of the Santa Lucia. It would have been dangerous, and well near impossible, except with horses well trained to such climbing. Even the pack mules born and bred in these mountains sometimes lose their footing, and tumble down the cañon sides, when too heavily loaded, to the destruction of their own lives and the contents of the pack. Many times the path lay over immense bowlders, where our horses had to choose their footing with the utmost care. It was necessary to use two cinches to hold our saddles in place. Sometimes the ascent was actually forty-five degrees, and I found it necessary to hold on to the front of the saddle to prevent falling backward. At times the saddle itself would seem almost to separate from the horse, as he made a steeper pull than usual, and I was fain to cling with one hand to his mane. Guidance was unnecessary, and an unwise interference with an animal that understood its business better than its rider did. There were places where the path turned in unexpected and acute angles, and places so steep in descent that I wished that mane grew behind, as well as before the saddle. At such places my feet were often on a level with my horse's ears, and I seemed to be sitting on his neck.

After the partial ascent of the first peak the view was magnificent, but there was little time to look backward or sidewise, for fear of being dragged off my horse by a pine limb, or having my eyes scratched out by the chapparal. Nature seemed rather indifferent to our admiration, and perhaps regarded man's invasion here in the light of hostility. Even my feet were not safe, for the trail sometimes became an incipient and roofless tunnel, from whose narrow sides projected threatening bowlders. Once Baptiste turned, and said something about *"mal camino"*; I knew little Spanish, but understood this intuitively, and answered, *"Si, senor,"* with energy. . . .

On the sides of many of the peaks were great stretches and clefts of bare reddish land, as though unfinished by Nature, or scarred by conflict. Nature is almost too absolute, too consciously triumphant here, and too fierce. She understands you, in an aloof and self-contained way, even too well, for she knows your secret; but she does not regard you as "a man and a brother," or admit you to confidence. You feel alien and shriveled. She is haughty and self-sufficient. If you have sinned she has no comfort for you, no sympathy with your fraility. She is something of Leonardo's Mona Lisa, -- she is the law of Moses.

Sometimes in the sunless depths of a cañon the trail would lead us to some gentler retreat, where a cool spring was surrounded by bending ferns, and graceful alders, and clumps of young redwoods. Here we would stop to breathe our horses, and drink from the spring; and as we watched the loosened leaves float down from the alders, soundless, and the dusky light in the tops of the redwoods, and the notched leaves of the fern above the still dark water of the spring, the peace of Nature fell upon us, and it was easy to understand how baffled and world-troubled spirits of all ages, and those too finely strung for the world's discords, have been drawn to such places as a refuge.

It was when emerging from such a cañon to the corresponding ridge that the ocean first burst upon us. Yet hardly the ocean itself, for it was entirely overlaid by a soft white haze. We were now actually at the top, an elevation of five thousand feet, and the descent began to be pretty rapid.

For the rest of the way the trail followed a pine-covered ridge. the cañons below were dark and green with redwoods. As we descended the short slopes the ocean was now and again lost to view, only to reappear through the framework of pines as we went forward on the alternating spurs of the ridge.

The animals seemed to have forgotten their weariness, and now traveled well as we were nearing their home. Finally, we came to the last descent, a great, rugged, gorge-broken series of declivities that formed the mountain side.

Below us lay the blue level of the ocean, from which the haze had lifted, the white, curving surf-line which was shut out by the cliffs directly in front, visible many miles on our left, far away to Point Gordo. The sun had set, and beyond the water lay great bands of rainbow colored mist. The ocean swelled and wrinkled in the dusky purple light. The unappeased crescendo of its long roar first broke far to the north, and was then slowly caught up and crashed from point to point past me, at last dying away to the south in far echoing and unreconciled regret. Then from the nearer caves the theme of the dying refrain arose again in subdued reverberations of unrest, swelled and went whispering through the caves in search of it knew not what, then died away again in accusing murmurs and low sea mutterings of its infinite discontent, -- leaving only the vague, heavy undertone of the deeper sea.

But where was *la casa*, my destination? I asked Baptiste. He pointed to a little hollow below a spur of the mountain side, where, half-smothered by trees, a small house was visible, lodged precariously on the mountain side, ready to slide to the sea three hundred feet below, should he of the seven-league boots give it a playful push with his toe.

I had ridden twenty miles, not to speak of the fifteen on the buckboard, and in spite of having rested myself by sitting my horse in various positions not taught by riding masters, I was glad to reach the end.

A continued sojourn here developed both advantages and defects. Human beings are so few that every character is individual and interesting. Nature, which was at first too untamed and overpowering, seemed to grow more gracious, although homely familiarity is still impossible, and attempts at close acquaintance are punished by soleless shoes and a humiliating sense of physical weakness.

Still, it is beautiful. Day by day the ocean sparkles under the sunbeams; the soft mist floats away up the gorges among the tops of the redwoods; the quails chatter and call from the cañons; the soft clouds form, and blend, and change, in the sky over the blue water; the white surf breaks languidly over the distant outlying rocks; the hawks dip, and circle, and pass, in the blue above; and the human heart falls into sympathy with this everlasting peace.

Were I a realist, I would tell of other things; of the ubiquitous *tocalote* which is so discouraging to pedestrian habits; of the inability to get to the top or to the bottom of anything; of the beach, which looks so near and is so far; or small gnats that pursue and bite like mosquitoes; of the too close proximity of cows and pigs; or a certain rooster who practices his newly learned crow near my window at 5 A.M. But I prefer watching the dusky shadows creep up the cañons,and the last glimpses of sunlight disappear from the ridges and die away on the white trunks of the sycamore trees; to see the sun himself drop behind the ocean, and the long bands of gold and purple form above his bed, as for canopy; to watch the red, and violet, and faint rose, fade from the sky, and the moon come up in the east.

As I write, the moon shines full on the water. Far out at sea a steamer glides past and fades away into the haze, leaving a faint black trail behind it. The light house glimmers from far San Simeon. The daylight is scarcely gone, and the pines stand black against the sky on the ridge above me. An owl calls from a tree near by. Just under the moon the water glints and shimmers into a thousand little silvery wrinkles. Farther away, where the swell of the ocean is visible, it lies in great satiny bands and curves, then fades away into blue and shadowy indistinctness, until it is lost in the far horizon.

II

The community is chiefly Spanish-Mexican -- a kind of driftwood from the wreckage of old California civilization. There are seven families, and in all about forty-five souls, counting the infants, a numerous class. Besides these there are a few unclassifiable characters, loose tag ends of the community, of various nationalities. There is a tall, loose-jointed Nova Scotian, who grew up among the scenes of Evangeline, and at present subsists on Mrs. Alexander's novels. There is a hermit called "Rocky," who lives in a lonely cañon, and has serious objection to tramps. When one appears he gets his gun, points to a mound and cross near by, signifying to the newcomer that there lies the last one, and advises him to "git."

Over the ridge is the log-built home of an old German, where at windy times you hear all day the lonesome creaking of a certain tall redwood leaning against another, and catch glimpses through the pines of white-caps dancing upon the dark blue of the ocean. Here he lives by himself in one room, his potatoes and onions in a straggling heap in one corner, his dog and his flour under the bed, and his fine-cut tobacco poured for convenience in an open tea box by the stove. He himself is a great, stooped clown, in dirty blue ducking, his colorless hair flying about in loose tags, his small, pale blue eyes half-blind and glassy with cataract, with a scraggy blond beard, and a great grinning mouth

stretched over large white teeth. He is a great reader of stories and of the press, although he must put the print within an inch of his eye in order to see. Oddly incongruous with himself is his scholarly knowledge of German. He detects your slightest error, and can untwist many a puzzling construction of Goethe and Schiller.

Across the cañon from the German lie the broad acres of the grand don of the community; a proud Castilian, a thinker, a philosopher, and a man of the world, suave, courteous, and diplomatic.

Even in this wild isolation there is the district school, a little terminal capillary in the great circulatory system of education, evidently in vital relation with the main currents, for a live county superintendent visits it once a year with enthusiasm and groans, -- the enthusiasm for the school, and the groans for the trip; for he is a heavy man, and not an accomplished horseman.

There are sixteen children enrolled, but where they come from would sadly puzzle the raw beholder of these unkempt mountains. If you ask one of the children where he lives, he will probably answer you, if he can muster sufficient English, "Oh, right down there," pointing indefinitely down the mountain side, -- by which he means a distance of perhaps three miles, which will seem six, if you walk it.

Most of the children, the few Americans included, speak Spanish with various degrees of fluency, and a very small degree of purity, while the English of the Mexican element is in most cases very lame and ludicrous. A few speak no English at all, and all the children of one family find it impossible to express themselves without the freedom of both languages. They will begin a statement in English, and finish it in Spanish, or vice versa, sometimes even changing from one to the other several times during a sentence. They chatter along in this mixture with perfect ease and unconsciousness.

Considering their opportunities the Spanish-Mexican children are bright. They are quick at writing, language, and mechanical arithmetic, though slower in reasoning than Americans. In disposition they are restless and quick- tempered, but for all that they are sensitive, affectionate, and appreciative of kindness; less helpless than American children, quite as cleanly, and courteous up to their lights.

The limited experience of the children of this community is astonishing. None of them ever saw a negro, a China-man, or a circus, or had a picture taken, and very few of them ever saw a church or a train. Several of them as old as fifteen years have never been away from the place, and have as much difficulty in imagining what a plain is like as did Walter Tell in Schiller's play. One little American boy of twelve begged his father to take him over the mountain to see a wagon.

The homes of these people are very primitive. When they wish to build a house they fell a redwood tree, split some shakes, and hew off a few young trees for joists and beams. With these they construct a house of from one to four rooms, and concoct some tables and bedsteads of what is left over. The patent furniture of the schoolhouse, including a heavy three-by-four table, was packed over on mule-back the forty miles from Kings City. Stove, chairs, provisions, and farming implements, are now all procured in the same way. While the lime kiln was in operation these things were brought by the schooner which landed at the kiln. The ranchers had then only to come with their mules and burros a few miles to claim their property and take it home. The kiln is said to have closed on account of mismanagement and failure to agree among the members of the company. It would seem that the mismanagement must have been gross to have prevented large profits, for it would be impossible to find a kiln more fortunately situated as to natural advantages. Three deep cañons unite, pour their waters together, and break through the rocky cliff into the ocean, forming a smooth sand beach and natural harbor. Great bowlders of calcareous rock of good quality gleam on the mountains from cliff and crag. When rock was needed the men climbed a few yards up the mountain side above the kiln, loosened a bowlder with crowbars, and sent it crashing down to where it was wanted. Fuel sufficient for years to come, and also lumber for barrel heads and hoops, is right at hand and owned by the company. A large sum of money has been sunk at this place. There are three large kilns and several well-built, substantial houses, besides the cottages for the workmen, which are so thickly strung along on either side of the road to the landing that the place has the appearance of a little town.

The operation of the kiln was naturally a great advantage to the community. Besides the convenience of supplies by schooner, the company paid a neighborhood carrier to bring the mail from Jolon,

a distance of thirty-five miles, at least once a week. Now, there is nothing certain or regular about its arrival, most of the residents receiving little mail and being indifferent about that little. It takes two days to go and come, and no one thinks of going merely for the mail, or seldom for anything less important than beans or tobacco. Sometimes, by good luck, you may get your papers and letters once a week for a while; and again it may happen to be three, and even four, weeks before you hear from the world and its vanities. If you are civilized, a general reader, and good correspondent, your mail will be brought to you at such times in a fifty-pound flour sack. If the San Antone and Nacimiento rivers get up, or the snow lies on the ridge, you may be cut off for six weeks or two months. In the meantime you live on scenery and beans. If you are wise, you will have Shakespeare, Emerson, and a few of the poets with you, -- you could hardly get enough novels to last. With these, and the great ocean in front of you with its human changefulness, the purple cañons about you with their elusive shadows, the birds and gray squirrels glancing about on sunny days, and the big mountains at your back, you can manage to exist, if you are on peaceful terms with yourself.

Nor is your human environment without interest. The Spanish-Mexicans are generous and kind-hearted, and above all happy and carefree. No extent of poverty seems to depress them. Last fall when the rain was so late in coming, the ranges had given out, the bones of starved cattle littered the hills, and the American rancheros wore faces like deacons, the Mexicans still carried their happy-go-lucky expressions.

They have, of course, the weaknesses of the social temperament. They all drink a little, and smoke a good deal. Sometimes they fall out with the Americans or with each other, but he who has the largest supply of tobacco is sure to have all his enmities made up during the first time of cut-off connection.

They are rather improvident, and only spasmodically industrious. They eat, drink, and are merry, think little of tomorrow and less of next year. If they have brown beans and coffee, and flour for tortillas, with an occasional pig or goat, they are satisfied. If they have potatoes, rice, and macaroni in addition, they are living in luxury. They care little for fruit or vegetables. The climate is perfect, and the soil in places well adapted to fruit and grapes, but they take little interest in trees or vines. They lack either the faith or the patience to plant and wait for slow returns. They raise some potatoes and beans, a little hay for their horses, and wheat for their chickens. The soil on the little hollows and slopes is a rich, light mold. This they turn up a few inches with a dull plow, sow, and scratch down with a home-made rake. What the birds and gophers leave does well, if it escapes being destroyed by the pigs and cattle that get in through carelessly made fences. It is not troubled by the goats and burros, which prefer thistles and sage brush.

The women of these families are more energetic and provident than the men. They often work in the field as well as in the house, and they all consider gardening and milking as exclusively feminine occupations as dishwashing. The washing and mending are always neatly done, and the Mexican homes are much more cleanly than those of Americans of the same grade.

Morally, these people are no worse and no better than American backwoodsmen anywhere without the restraint of education and public opinion. I doubt whether to credit their race type with quite the degree of frankness that is characteristic of the Anglo-Saxon, but of the cruelty often attributed to them I see no evidence.

Their religion is, of course, Roman Catholic. You will find cheap prints of the Virgin in their bedrooms, and generally a tiny crucifix by the rude little crib of the youngest child. They try to get "out," -- that is, over the mountains, to have their babies christened by a priest, and some of the older children have been baptized where their parents were married, in the old San Antone Mission, now falling to decay.

Family affection among them is strong, and a new baby seems always to be welcome. Children learn to work and become helpful early. Girls of thirteen often do most of the housework for a large family, and it is not uncommon to see a *muchacho* of five or six sent alone on horseback to a neighbor several miles distant. In fact, the boys learn to ride as soon as they can walk and talk, and as soon as they can throw a riata they are seen practicing on the goats and calves about. To ride well, to dance well, to throw the lasso with dexterity, and incidentally to speak a little English, is the ambition of all Mexican boys, and one they seldom fail to realize. If the ability to play the accordeon or strum a guitar is added, it is as the finishing touch of an already satisfactory education. The power to make love gracefully goes without saying, as it is a faculty born with them. A raw young vaquero in sombrero and overalls will often astonish you with a compliment and bow that would do credit to one of McAllister's four hundred. They fall in love easily, get broken hearts, go careening over the country on a pet mustang at fifty miles a day, break a few broncos, participate in a rodeo, attend a fandango, smile into another pair of eyes, and are well again.

Sometimes, of course, they are jealous, and there is the glitter of knives and a more serious *denouement*, but this happens generally only under the influence of liquor and in cities where there is no room for wild rides and spacious atmosphere.

The air of romance we associate with the Spanish-Mexicans is not a creation of fiction. They have the artistic, impressionable temperament of the Latin races, are warmer blooded than we Anglo-Saxons, more restless, loving the extremes of indolence and wild exercise, hating above all things care and routine.

There is often a kind of brigandish dash and grace in the pose of some grizzled, bepatched, middle-aged Mexican, that reminds you of pictures of Italian bandits; and indeed, you feel while in this community, that you are living in an unreal world, where the people are pictures, vanishing views of a life foreign and alien to ours.

There is a certain pathos in their situation. They are poor, and most of them are growing poorer. They will tell you that before the *Americanos* came the grass on the open spaces of the mountains reached their horses' necks, the cattle were always fat, and they themselves had plenty of money and good clothes, and ate their melons and tamales in the shade without a care, and never did a stroke of work out of the saddle. The Americans came in, took advantage of their ignorance of land laws, overstocked the remaining government land, which had been used in common, crowded them into narrower quarters, sold them brass jewelry for gold, and cheated them generally. It is not strange that they have a feeling of bitterness toward us.

With the help of the school, and the experience of work among Americans in the towns and valleys of Monterey, the younger generation are becoming Americanized, and learning the adaptability of the modern Californian; but the old folks stay on the ranch, and eat beans and tortillas, and have as little variety in their social life as in their diet.

They have no general community life whatever. There is sometimes a picnic, sometimes a fandango, when Mexican friends come from places twenty-five miles distant, where a good deal of whiskey is drunk, and many hot tamales eaten, and where the *borrego* (or sheep dance) and other fantastic steps alternate with the modern waltz and quadrille until broad daylight in the morning. Sometimes two or three beeves are killed, and the guests invited to stay for a second, and sometimes for a third night. But these protracted fandangos are now very rare. The people are too poor to have them. I was for a while a spectator of one that lasted all night. All ages from twelve to sixty were on the floor, and all danced with enthusiasm. It was very merry; a trifle free and easy, and a bit noisy; but with the exception of their peculiar dances and the unconcealed drinking, there was little that might not have occurred at a middle class society party.

Looked at from the outside, the lives of these people seem very barren. But I remember a little grave on a hillside where the white carnations are overrun with wild buttercups and baby-blue-eyes, and recall a Mexican mother by the little cross; and I reflect that they have the experiences which make up life everywhere, -- friendships, jealousies, love affairs, dissipations, broken hearts, marriage, and the mystery of life and death.

Most of these Mexicans lived formerly near old Monterey, or nearer the center of Monterey County, but have gradually removed to these scarcely accessible

wilds, where another westward move would be into the ocean. Twenty years ago there was but one family here, a Mexican nucleus. Then a few years later came a large American family of the Joseph Smith branch of Mormons. Two daughters of the family, marrying stray Americans who found their way hither, increased the community by additions of numerous children. Later, several Spanish-Mexican families arrived. The place still looks so wild that it seems as though it might have been settled last year, but the ranchers tell you that it looked different when they came. The whole mountain side was covered with an impenetrable tangle of underbrush, and the slopes and ridges with forests of pine. They are still fighting the former with fire and grub-hoe, and the latter with axes, with as yet no appearance of brilliant success. The trails near the beach when neglected for a year become impassable and almost undiscoverable, so rapidly does the underbrush grow.

As late as eight years ago deer were as tame and almost as numerous as the cattle. It was nothing unusual to see them in herds of fifteen, and to see forty or fifty in the course of a day's ride. They were frequently seen about the barns eating scattered hay with the cattle, and a few became quite gentle. But their indiscriminate slaughter, and the sale of their flesh at prohibited seasons under the name of

beef, has greatly thinned them. Even yet, however, you can seldom ride over the mountains without seeing several, and they often stand and look at you, or go on grazing, apparently without fear.

Other wild animals have disappeared correspondingly. Cats, foxes, and coyotes are still plentiful, but the California lion is now rarely seen. Six and eight years ago both bears and lions prowled about the houses of the settlers, preying upon their goats and pigs. Several of the Mexicans show skins of lions which they killed with their knives to prevent their dogs from getting the worst of an impromptu fight. On one occasion an old Mexican found himself armed only with a riata when his dogs had chased a lion up a tree. He stopped, lifted off his serape, took a look at the animal, and proceeded to lasso it. Catlike, the creature watched as the lasso circled about the thrower's head. In a flash the thong had whizzed through the air to its aim. the lion jumped, luckily on the off side of the limb, and hung itself.

The dexterity of the Mexican and Spanish in the use of the riata is equaled only by their originality in its application. Near an old adobe home on the inland side of these mountains is a great rocky mesa, a kind of cleavage some hundred feet high, covered on top with mescal and chamisal brush. The men of the family were coming on horseback from a cattle hunt, and going toward the cliff from the upper side, when the dogs from the house startled a lion which had been skulking in a ditch near by. The animal made for the cliff, ran directly up its rugged perpendicular sides, and left the dogs howling below. The men galloped up to the edge of the cliff, swung their riatas, and drew dog after dog to the top. As each one came up it staggered about for a few seconds, and then was off with a howl on the track of the lion, which an hour later was shot and carried home.

New as this region apparently is, it has at one time been far more thickly inhabited than at present. The soil of the high slopes next to the ocean is full of the remains of abalone and mussel shells carried there by Indian settlements, and flint knives and arrow heads are found in abundance. Certain caves in the mountains show traces which prove that the Indians have been scattered all the way from the San Antonio Mission to the coast. One in particular, a kind of level excavation in a ledge of sandstone, which is so large that several dozen horses take refuge under it in stormy weather, shows the smoke-stains from their fires, and curious little excavations apparently used as receptacles for water or food.

Although these mountains seem so undeveloped, the immediate community of which I write can hardly expand to any great extent. To the north and the south the range is owned by a few large ranchers, the lime kiln company own the most and best near by, and the rich flats and foothills of the eastern slope comprise one large grant owned by a company in San Francisco. In between these ranches is a good deal of scattered government land, good in spots, but the good spots are not large enough to pay to file on them for stock ranching purposes.

There has been an immense deal of money made in these mountains, but cattle raising has seen its best days, even on the larger ranches. The ranges have of late years been constantly overstocked, and the feed has greatly decreased in quantity. If one has a large ranch, stays on it, looks after his cattle, and manages well, he can still make money, but he cannot make it in the indolent fashion of former days, when great tracts of government land were free grazing range, and cattle owners were far between.

If these mountains are ever more thickly settled than at present, it will become possible only through a change of occupation to fruit and vine culture, and this in turn waits a nearer railroad, of which there is no prospect unless the Los Burros mines to the south, or the recently discovered coal ledge to the north, should develop beyond expectation, in which case connection might be made coastwise.

So far as soil and climate are concerned there is no reason why fruit and grapes cannot be raised here as well as in the Santa Cruz mountains. Already near the town of Jolon I saw a settler clearing out the chapparal to plant a prune orchard, and farther west in the mountains, up the cañon of the Nacimiento, an enterprising city man has found a rich school section, on which he is beginning a walnut grove.

But a railroad is not likely to pierce the Santa Lucia direct for several centuries. A better hope for the Rockland community is through water connection, which they themselves might make possible could they be made to understand the advantages of cooperation. Should they all turn to fruit culture, establish a cannery, a wine-press, and drying facilities, still reserving their more mountainous range for live stock, they could easily induce schooners to land regularly, and ship their produce. But the average backwoodsman, whether American or Mexican, does not spend his days seeing or hearing or practicing some new thing. Ignorance is notoriously afraid of cooperation. . . . It is altogether probable that the community will remain preserved, fossilwise, in the sediment of its present peculiarities for some time to come.

## III

After spending several months in this place I one day made ready to return to civilization. My baggage was strapped on a mule, and over the blue mountains and down the rocky trails we went, with magnificent sweeps of horizon and glorious atmosphere, --my dark chaperone, our young vaquero, and myself. Twenty miles over the mountains, and we dropped, as it were, from the sky into the meadow below, and were at the home of Anselmo, a century-old adobe.

The next day we laid over. As I remember it the day is a vision of alternating wild rides and lazy dreams under big oaks --of silver glimpses of salmon in clear streams, alder shadowed and sun-flecked, --of mad gallops over brush and ditch after bands of sleek horses and runaway cows, -- of an April sun mistily aslant over sandstone cliffs, crowned atop with the spotted stalks of the mescal, -- of acres of odorous blue lupin, filled with the hum of bees, -- of a rest in this by the side of a panting horse, -- of an odorous dusk, and a dash home in the starlit night.

The next morning it rained -- a soft April rain, a mere caress for the flowers. The grass was gray with it, and the air was like velvet. Again we mounted and were off, with fresh horses and pack mule. The road was soon good -- level for miles. We longed for a gallop, but our mule was "bronco," and refused to lead well. We soon devised a plan. My chaperone and I rode behind, shouting and brandishing our shawls. Off he went on a gallop, we following like mad through field and across creek for several miles until the San Antonio Mission appeared.

Here we dismounted and gathered apple blossoms from a scraggy survivor of the old Mission orchard, and made bouquets of the fragrant Castilian roses, hanging deep colored and dewy by the old walks and tumble-down walls. An earthy and antiquated smell pervades the old building. We groped through the dark corridors and stumbled over broken tiles. Half the roof has fallen in, and lies piled up on the floor of the audience room. A walk through the long arches, a look at the graves, and soon we mounted and were off again through the dewy air for Jolon; and the last picture I have connected with my stay in the Santa Lucia is a scared pack mule a-gallop with a shaking pack of valises, boxes of books, and bristling umbrellas, ourselves swaying around curves, and ducking under trees in jolly pursuit.

Lillian Bos Ross

*A thousand words a day and bread to bake*

*Lillian Bos Ross (1890--1960) first glimpsed the Big Sur coast in 1924 when she and Harry Dick Ross explored on foot the blank stretch of map between Hearst Castle and Monterey. They fell in love with the land. It was not until 1939 that an opportunity arose to caretake Beth Livermore's cabin at Lime Creek, but during the intervening years, when the Rosses lived among the Telegraph Hill group of writers and artists, and later in Salinas, she kept her memory of Big Sur alive.*

*Living a pioneer life at Livermore Ledge, Shanagolden (as her friends called her) immersed herself in the land and the legends of the south coast. Entirely self-educated, with only a few years of grammar school education, she determined to develop her natural talent as a story teller. With her husband's support, and with the encouragement of her friend Carl Sandburg, she began to work seriously, setting herself a writing schedule of a minimum of 1,000 words a day. From April 28, 1937, when she first sat down at the old Royal typewriter, until spring of 1940, Shanagolden turned out columns for the Salinas and Carmel papers. Then on June 1, 1940, she began writing her Big Sur novel. The first draft was completed in four months, the final draft submitted for publication in 1941, and a contract signed on April 28, 1942, exactly five years after she put her first words on paper. The Stranger became a best seller and was later made into the movie, "Zandy's Bride." All of this, while simultaneously baking bread, milking the cow, planting a garden, making cheese and leading the busy social life characteristic of that period in Big Sur.*

*By the time The Stranger was published, the Rosses were living high up on an isolated observation post as spotters for the Air Warning Service. "The solitude is glorious," she said to an interviewer. "It is the most unlonely place I've ever been. We see very few people, but the work is so interesting, the situation so dramatically beautiful, Harry Dick and Chiquita (the Ross's pet wire-haired terrier) such good companions, it has never occurred to me to think that anyone would be lonely here."*

*The Rosses built a house on Partington Ridge, with a studio where Harry Dick worked at sculpting and Lillian continued to write daily. A second Big Sur novel, Blaze Allen, was published and a third in process when she began to suffer from what we now know as Alzheimer's disease. She died at Agnew State Hospital in 1960.*

*What fueled this remarkable woman who accomplished with such seeming ease what so many struggle to achieve? In her own words, "...the only thing humans have control of is themselves. There is no way to avoid the strange twists and turns in our lives, but we are absolute masters of our own reactions to them. Therefore, no one is so poor, so remote from opportunity that they cannot take the stuff of daily life and with it, put quality into themselves."*

# Diary of a Walk on the Old Coast Trail, 1924

## by Lillian Bos Ross

*Monday, July 21, 1924*

Left our beloved Barranca on San Simeon Beach at 11 am after writing a farewell note to the Mysterious Maker of Rubber Sausages who had occupied the Slaughter House before us -- also a note to Sebastian Villa, cow-boy extra-ordinary. The note said "They are not long -- the days of wine and roses. I kiss my fingertips to you. Adios." He will like that, I think. We were picked up and taken 22 miles on the road by a gold miner located on Salmon Creek. He is getting $2.50 to the ton and mining out one and a half tons a day. Spent Mon. night at Salmon Creek where we caught trout for our dinner and breakfast. Made a bed of blue lupin boughs on the side of the trail.

*Tuesday morning*

Slept wonderfully--in the morning swam in the deepest greenest coldest pool below the fall. Harrydick finds his shoe a cripple and turns cobbler with a piece of fishing twine and the pliers he found. We finally got away and located the trail at 10 am. It started straight up and kept it up. Certainly a gruelling uphill trek. Ate lunch at a whispering spring and dinner in a wonderful clearing by a deserted cabin with a tumble-down fireplace. Saw nine deer. A mile out (and up) lost the trail and found -- a bull! An inquisitive bull with no stout fence to stay his investigations. HD hid me behind a rock pile and told me to remember all the bull stories I could to keep Mr. Bull amused, and HD would hunt the trail. There was nothing to climb but a mountain, and no place for the bull to toss us but into the sea. HD found the trail and we lost the bull.

*Wednesday*

Lunch at Villa Creek. Took wrong trail and lost two hours and four miles. Bad luck. But at 3 pm we sighted Krinkle's (Krenkel is correct spelling). Saw 3 deer threatening their corn patch -- and my own ideas were not orthodox -- but the respectable HD saved the patch -- but he stole two peaches -- near gold mine Blue Jay #2. At Krenkel's we found a warm welcome and rested a couple of hours. These people have been located there 35 years. Found, after an hour, that one of the little boys -- 8 and 10 -- was named Lillian. She wore overalls and a cap like her brother and was busy dragging around traps. A queer, rambling place with beds in every room -- 9 children, a grapevine 19 years old wanders all over outdoors and has tons of grapes.

They grow everything -- grapes, peaches, cantaloupe, melons, apples, walnuts, oranges, plums, berries -- every sort of vegetable. Always have a buck deer swinging in the smoke house. We bought liberally and started away at 4 pm headed for Willow Creek five miles away. Got lost a dozen times and brought up at every gold mine in the hills. Nicest one was the Gilded Clown. Found Willow Creek at 7:20 -- dead tired -- lame -- hungry -- and a hard place to make camp. HD felled two trees and wove us a bough bed and the stream soon sang us to sleep.

*Thursday*

Woke late, dawdled over breakfast and breaking camp but were off about 10:30. Went through magnificent pine forest -- cathedral quiet and fragrant as frankincense. Then up the worst grade yet -- loose shale rock -- a sun that felt for your neck and your nose -- and God, God how tired and hot when we sighted the sea. HD had been "rock hunting" for quail. When he saw the bay he said, "let's just hole in here for the day -- or forever!" I agreed. HD named this bit of loveliness "The Bay of the Fishing Pelicans." We built a fireplace and were at home. We started to fish Willow Creek but at the first hole we gasped -- tore off our clothes and dived. Such a swimming hole! And a copper-colored snake came and swam with us and a fireball that everyday folk call a hummingbird. And I kissed my lover long and long as he lay on the smooth, hot rock of untold antiquity. Gleaming white among the rocks and trees we were the first man and woman -- and the birds and fish were not afraid of us. We built a gorgeous fire to keep the copper of the sunset before us. In the morning the fire was still smoking. We left at 7:30 in the morning, bound for Gorda about three miles away.

*Friday*

First interesting thing was a generously large deserted house. Used to be post office at Gorda. Found a 1915 Century Magazine with pictures of Lewis Carroll and Alice in Wonderland. Two men rode up -- they were driving cattle -- a Spaniard who had some magnificent spurs he had made. The other man named Mansfield said he "had a right to keep the Home Place for four years." Thought we might buy some tea at the Home Place. We were eager to see this so loved Home Place. Such desolation -- dirt, no curtains -- no yard, a pile of deer horns and deer bones on the dirty stoop -- a biting bitch called Dixie -- two utterly "blah" women -- one a Mexican with affectations, the other a red-headed hussy. Neither one knew if they could sell us anything -- they couldn't ride -- they didn't know how far it was from or to anything. They gave us a little packet of green tea, however. We asked some men who were haying for the directions to a log house where we were told by Mrs. Krenkel we might buy something. They offered HD a job -- refused. We found the log house and the backbone of the nation. The kindliest, friendliest man and dog -- who stopped his fence building and took us to his house. A one-room log affair -- great big room, no windows. Flooring hand-hewed and each board three inches thick. Wife deaf -- clean. Pretty baby -- clean -- had just been bathed and dressed. Named Warren -- 5 months. One other child, Lloyd; scrappy kitten I called Firpo. We bought bread -- 15 cents. The lady gave us a jar of honey. They had turkeys, cow, chickens -- nice folk. Then we were off to Mill Creek -- six miles distant. Had lunch on Wild Cattle Creek on a bank of green moss and maidenhair fern where a cunning little wood mouse went about his business. I fished and caught two trout. So HD started. He caught five and I one more. A good lunch -- and then away again at 2:40 pm. Hot uphill, shale trail. Dragged into Mill Creek at 5:40, found it a big creek, but on a hog ranch. Hard to find a place to camp. Bed early, the hogs came in the night and stole our beans.

*Saturday*

Up at 5 and grabbed our packs and away before breakfast. Soon sighted a clean bunk house and a barn. Found one man who sent us to the ranch house to see if we could buy food. He was surprised that we were about so early. Got to the house, woman not up. Heard strange voices and eagerly detained us. Sold us a big piece of home cured bacon for 25 cents. Sent us on to her aunt at the post office called Lucia where she said we could buy things. We were looking for a good place to cook breakfast. Found it about 8:30 am at Lime Kiln Creek. Utterly beautiful. This time I said, "Let's spend the day." I washed the towels -- my socks, underwear -- our hair -- baths -- a swim in a deep pool -- good fishing -- sunshine among the redwoods. About 10:30 two Harlan boys rode by. The big one -- Fred -- let me get on his horse. Had one horse, colt, very wild. The other boy, Marion, was breaking him. They said they would be back between 4 and 5 pm and would bring one extra saddle horse, and also take our packs up the hill. They came -- I rode Mable -- a buckskin packed our luggage. HD walked. A long two and a half miles of steep wooded beautiful trail -- then on an overhanging shelf the trail wound by the sea. We got there in time for supper. We slept in the redwoods by a spring and reported at the Harlan's for breakfast at 7:30 the next morning.

*Sunday*

Called by a horn made of kelp -- hurried to breakfast of oatmeal and cream, good coffee, corn cakes made of home ground corn meal raised on the place with honey from their bees, eggs, and apricot sauce, creamed potatoes, jellie and white napkins. We stayed talking until 9:30, bought eggs, bread, salt, potatoes, onions, walnuts, butter, were given a squash and a powder horn and four meals, charged $2.30. We walked to Vicente Creek in time for lunch through country so steep and hot that I was so weary that I had a hysterical crying spell as I lay on the moss. Rested two hours and at 2:30 were off to Devil's Gulch. Passed through some beautiful redwood country and saw the sort of butterflies you see in jeweler's windows. Saw 3 deer of a new specie -- gray ones -- beautiful. Have had a few thimble-, goose- and huckleberries, and fish and watercress off the country. Found Devil's Gulch a terror to get into -- could hear the creek roaring an hour before we got to it. Wild lovely creek with lots of water. HD sent me early to bed in a deep soft bed of redwood branches. Slept well. Went to bed with the plan to trek out before breakfast for Big Creek, a couple of miles away.

*Monday*

Awoke at twenty to seven. I hurried down to the creek and had a bath and swim while HD had a cigarette and a front row seat at the show. We shouldered our packs and forty-five minutes later were at Big Creek. We had a fine breakfast and HD caught two trout and the fishing fever while I got breakfast. He cut a pole and fixed my line while I did dishes and put some beans to bake in the hot stones. I went up and HD down stream to fish. Found many traces of cougar and bear. Caught seven trout with a bit of red leaf from a flower. HD caught 17. I fried them all for dinner in butter. Had 8 left to carry with us. We left Big Creek at 10 of 3 and it took us an hour and ten minutes to get out of the canyon. Some of the most marvelous views on the trip though. Mountains piled one on top of the other. Great rocks and caves, and then miles up, great gold pastures of wild grass, and blue, blue sky. Out we traveled as fast as we could along a crumbling ledge 2000 feet above the sea, with a sheer drop to the rocks below. Saw an abalone fisherman. Made Rat Canyon at 5:30 and HD found us a beautiful camp with a private waterfall and a four poster bed made of giant redwoods. Deer came to drink among the maidenhair ferns that fringed the pool. HD's poison oak is getting better. To bed at 7:30 and watched the star lighter hang out all his little lamps. Plans to be up early.

*Tuesday*

Woke at 5:15. Packed and away 3 minutes of 6. The sun was already hot as we climbed out of the canyon. At the top we looked across green redwoods and a mountain side ablaze with Indian paint brush, goldenrod, morning glories, columbine, wild honeysuckle -- the red of poison oak and Indian cherries -- blue, grey, purple and yellow lupin -- ferns -- a riot of color and it has been so all the way. We had breakfast at a dinky sort of watering hole of a creek -- good breakfast of bacon, eggs, camp bread, honey and tea. Picked wild gooseberries. Then on the march again at 9 o'clock. Got off the road at a deserted ranch clearing -- taking a rather broad well-marked trail. It soon dwindled out and we found ourselves in an impasse. Straight cliff to ocean on one hand -- deep crevasse in front -- climb a mountain without a trail through thistles, nettles and thorn bushes or -- go back! We went up. Damn tuff -- I swore enough to fry me another million years. We at last got on the trail after an hour of blistering sun and nettle stings, and found we were about a mile from a prosperous looking farm. Stopped there -- found everyone was in the haying. Presently an apparition with a high tummy and a broad ass wearing spurs and a sun bonnet and a respectable chin whisker -- approached. In a deep, brisk and business-like tone it greeted us, taking off the sun bonnet as it spoke, and twas a femme! She strode about her sparkling aluminum furnished kitchen in men's pants and men's shirt and shoes -- and the window curtains were white and starched. We bought bread, coffee, eggs and honey for a dollar -- and were away to find a place to lunch -- and with Anderson Canyon as our objective for the night. Eight miles away. Lunch on a dirty side hill near a nice stream. A Spanish boy rode by just as we had finished. He was one of the Berrandos (Boronda is the correct spelling)
-- there are some families of that name scattered about. We packed and were away again at 2:35. Saw a beautiful doe and twin fawns -- watched them for some minutes. Most graceful. At 3:45 we wound down into Anderson's Gulch -- and there by a water fall of four falls we camped. Our bed is up on a shelf 50 feet above our fire -- at about the level of the first fall. Our fire is at the base of the third fall. HD is catching trout for supper. I am tending the fire and cooking beans and polenta. The woods are green, still and sweet.

*Diary courtesy of Harry Dick Ross*

*I am proud of this neighbor of mine. Her transition from a high-powered life in San Francisco to a remote mountain cabin on the south coast of Big Sur has not been easy. She is still hanging in there.*

# The Long Walk–a Rite of Passage

## by Judith Goodman

The timing was right. Holly was ready to leave San Francisco and her stressful life as manager of a downtown boutique when the man popped the question: how would she like to come and live with him in his cabin in the Big Sur hills? After seven years of non-stop motion, the idea had instant appeal. To get off the treadmill and meet the challenge of a totally different life. . . something inside answered YES.

The man presented no problem. She had been fond of him for several years; she knew him for a good man. True, up until then he had been one of many, but why not try this other way that people call monogomy.

Holly is careful and matter-of-fact. Knowing herself and her cycles, she made a clear agreement with the man. For one year, from September, 1982 until the same date in September, 1983, she committed to making her home in the south coast cabin. Sight unseen!

Holly thought she knew what life in Big Sur would be like, having visited Lincoln on the north coast before: lunch in Carmel with the girls, drinks with friends at Fernwood -- like moving from the city to the suburbs. "I didn't know I was moving to the wilderness" -- 2500 feet above the sea, in the middle of nowhere, no neighbors for miles around, seventy miles from the nearest town. "It was a shock."

The transition was hard. Like withdrawing from a drug, Holly kept returning to San Francisco for a city injection every two weeks. She threatened to leave every time things got rough. "I felt sorry for my roommate; he had to listen to a lot of garbage." She had never done any kind of physical work before, never had a garden, never done her own laundry. "I used to take it out to a Chinese laundry. I asked Lincoln where's the laundromat? He showed me the tub in the backyard."

After only a month of this new life, while Lincoln was trying patiently to teach her to transplant cabbages, Holly lost her

44

patience. She could not stand to be here one more minute.

*So I stamp off in very dramatic style, and all I have on is a tee shirt and a pair of pants and little flat shoes -- get into my car and drive off -- a very dramatic exit. You know, it was more for the drama than anything else -- I never really intended to drive as far as I drove, but I was angry and I had no idea of the time that had passed as I was driving south on the Coast Ridge Road. I just kept driving and driving and fuming, "I gotta get away" -- and pretty soon the sun is setting and it's getting late and I'm still on this road. I don't want to turn around because the road has been so bad -- after awhile it isn't maintained anymore -- what I want to do is find some way to get to Highway One and around. So I keep driving -- looking for a sign that says Highway One -- well, there were signs that said Highway One, but underneath were little symbols BIKE AND HIKERS ONLY, so I keep driving and driving. Then all of a sudden I see a Highway One sign, I turn abruptly into it and the road ends and I just fall into a pit -- it was a little trail over the hill -- if you had a dirt bike you might have made it. Walking would be better or a donkey.*

*So here I am stuck. I have no idea how long I've driven, where I am or anything. I have no blanket, no food, no flashlight, nothing. Dark is setting in. As far as I remember it was right before or right after new moon, but it was dark, maybe a little star reflection. So the only thing I could think of to do -- here I'd been in the area for a month, and at the time my fears were more of being found there -- having some Trapper John or somebody coming up to me and finding me there would freak me out more than if I just got on the road and fled the scene, so I opt to do that. I walked home. I think from looking at the map later, that it was*

*about eighteen or twenty miles. I have these flat shoes on and my toe- nails went through my feet in walking down the hills and my feet were all bloody and I was freezing cold. It took me about six to eight hours to walk home.*

In the morning Holly knew that she must choose. She could leave Big Sur and give up this new life, or she must make a real commitment to do what it takes to be here. Holly decided to stay:

*This time I'm going at it with a different sort of attitude. It was that experience that did it. I realized that for the first time in my life my survival rested on me. There was no one there to help me. I had to rely on my own resources, and it was an invigorating experience to feel that. It wasn't the type of survival that you feel in the city -- a threat of rape or murder. It was a different type of survival, it was against nature, not against man. I'd never been challenged like that before and I felt it was worth the experience of living here.*

Holly's one year commitment has come and gone; her trial year included the worst winter in Big Sur history when Highway One fell into the sea and isolation became complete. Holly is still here, enjoying the new experience of life in the wilderness, meeting the challenges of the simple life.

# Poems

## by Melissa Blake

*Melissa and her husband, Charlie Levitsky, came to Big Sur to visit, and like so many others, fell in love with the life here, and stayed to make it their home. A former dancer and choreographer, she has been a poet all her life.*

*"I started writing poetry when I was about 9. A friend of mine who also wrote suggested we have a contest; we must each write a poem about a flower. I wrote one, and she wrote this one: POPPY /A daughter of the Gods /Tall and divinely fair. I gave up instantly and she won the contest, as I had to admit I had never thought of anything like that. Many years later I read the same lines, or similar, by a better known poet than my friend, and decided she was an even better reader than writer.*

*My next venture was to send 3 poems to a contest by Nebraska's Poet Laureate, whose works I hated, and whose name I have forgotten. I wrote to annoy him, but one of the judges thought my poems were pretty good for a 13 year old, and sent them to Harriet Monroe, at POETRY magazine. For some unknown reason she published one of them.*

*Being an arrogant (and ignorant) youngster, I thought to myself, "If it's as easy as that to be published, why should I bother?"*

*I never sent out another poem until we came to live in Big Sur. I found it was not that easy."*

WINTER STORM WITH WHALES (Whale Haiku)

January sky --
Whales hurry past, having missed
The winter solstice.

Black storm-blurred rocks -- near,
Only cormorants and whales
Are comfortable.

Sleet grey slants of rain --
But whales make no distinction,
Spouting the same way.

A glowering sky --
Schools of whales rollick along,
Fat, warm and playful.

A tidal wave -- no,
The sea floor is rising up!
A whale draped in kelp.

THEATRICAL WINTER SOLSTICE

Cardboard redwoods indent for depth
The cyclorama of canyon walls
While cypress tantalizers edged in scrim
Of lace vine clusters adorned by birds
Present, as if for Midsummer Eve,
King Oak, replete with mistletoe crown.

But beyond the rocks,
Beyond the skip rope of foam flung,
Beyond the ignorant bawling of the surf,
Whales are lolloping south and spouting
Out of their blunt heads, banging the flat sea
With their black tails.

CONSCIOUSNESS ASSUMING THE FORM OF A CRANE

(after Morris Graves)

A crane balances on the kelp bed
his far out raft is tipping
the false sea-lions' heads
bobbing and inviting rocking

Watch and he will not

Poised on a pivot
universal joint
of tipping space
his silhouette
proclaims
consciousness unwavering
on the tricky raft
adjusting itself
to the being and becoming.

THE FITNESS OF THE ENVIRONMENT

Blue herons belong in the rushes
A rabbit enhances the bushes
And water's becoming to fishes
But a king snake is ringed among squashes
Stretching out his black and cream meshes
Between warty crooknecks and sleek calabashes.

FOSSIL

Claws, beak, skeleton bland
Light to the hand
Fifty million years of time
Wither leather wings to lime
Precessions of creatures crawl toward death
Sharing the hollowhood of breath
Opossums' bare reptilian tails
Still drag across the redwood trails
The trilobite's descendant, dull
Pillbug rolling into ball
Affirms that forms are seldom lost
Iguana's spine bears dragon's crest
And coal-beds where these patterns rest
Are filled with fern fronds, black, embossed.

## THE SEVERAL ADVANTAGES OF LIVING UNDER A TIN ROOF

It doesn't leak:
Mist fizzles on it
Showers indent its corrugated keyboard
Hail hundred dozen jackhammers it
Wind wrinkles it
Hurricane shakes it like a rug.

Branches scrape questions on it
Leaves ping pong, then skate down it
Buds shotgun it.

Cat claws slatepencil it
Bird feet tickle code on it
Sun warms it;
Friends pebble signal on it.

## HANDYMAN

That tardy handyman has finally trimmed the topiary bay trees
Daubed clear varnish on the best new poison oak leaves
Raided the cricket's sewing basket for thimble flowers
Basted a few fresh tassels on cypress branches
Replenished the cadmium orange on Indian paint brushes
Squirted lemon oil in sticky cups of yuccas
Wound up clockwork tarantulas, heading them hillward on highways
Lit the blue flames of the ceanothus
Set the buzzards wheeling in slow counter-circles
And so -- well, here it is again:
Springtime.

## FELLOW TRAVELER

Wait, lizard -- don't run away
You and I sun ourselves
On slate colored rocks, on serpentine
Sun and invite our souls ....
Presuming we have souls.
We are in identical situations
Within the universe.
It behooves us to behave well to each other.

SONG OF THE WHITE ANT

*I warm my hands before the fire*
*And sometimes turn my back*
*While termites in the cypress log*
*Change from white to black.*

*If we should burn in atom's blaze*
*Earth's surface glaze to glass*
*Will God benignly warm his hands?*
*Or merely burn his ass?*

RACCOONS OF THE WORLD

*Velvet-masked waddle-paced bandit on witch-dwindled hands,*
*Why this cackle-snaffle group quarrel?*
*Ignorant -- better, innocent -- of hero conditioning,*
*United you can easily burgle*
*Any man-made mechanical fastening*
*And glut on fanciful gourmet comestibles.*

*What do you care for opposable thumbs?*
*Ring-tailed hump-backed wondercat!*
*Bread-rinser!*

BAT

*Twitch corner tumble dip of dainty leather, dart!*
*Gauze glider in gingerly gloom*
*Blood snatcher, breath sucker, hair tweaker! (Scream)*

*Ebony-congo-idol-faced fur-bearer*
*Web-fingered collapsible umbrella hanger*
*Cavern swooper, sonar squeaker, hole haunter!*

*Drop. tingling leaves, from your evening eaves,*
*Bless the crepuscular light with your transparent*
*Muscular flight.*

# Photographs
*by Pat Addleman*

*Olympia*

# *A Day in the Life of a Big Sur Woman*

Lynda Sargent in a beam of sunlight

# Letters from Pinyon Peak

## by Lynda Sargent

*If solitude is the greatest challenge offered by life in Big Sur, Lynda Sargent has faced it most directly. In these letters to Harry Dick and Shanagolden Ross written while Lynda was fire-watch on Pinyon Peak, she speaks eloquently of how it feels to see "a total of seven human faces in four months."*

*Born in Henniker, New Hampshire, in 1897, daughter of an unsuccessful farmer, Lynda Sargent taught school briefly before her marriage to a Harvard law professor. She divorced him in Reno in 1934. It was on this trip west that she first visited California, and fell in love with Carmel. Within a year she had moved west, rented a house in Carmel, hired a maid and joined the circle of writers and artists then gathered there.*

*Lynda found her way to Big Sur in the late 30's, seeking a quiet place where she could write. She rented the Log House, now part of Nepenthe, and quickly became an active member of the community of creative spirits living on the coast. Lynda did write, but as she explains, she was much too busy living to focus on her writing. As her friend Henry Miller sees her failure to complete her novel-in-progress, "Lynda had everything that goes to make a writer except that one indispensable thing -- belief in oneself." In the eyes of her nephew, Richard French, the fatal flaw was that there was always a man to take her mind off her work. Whatever the problem, Lynda was a prolific but unpublished writer until 1976 when French found a publisher for her Gothic novel* Judith Duquesne.

*In 1956, between men and somewhat disenchanted with the Big Sur scene, Lynda took a job with the US Forest Service as fire-watch on Pinyon Peak. Later, she took over the Chews Ridge lookout, and in the early 1960's married Fred Tuttle, also fire-watch at Chews Ridge. Summers, they spent at the lookout together; winters at Cachagua in Carmel Valley. After Tuttle's death, she lived with her nephew Richard French until senile dementia made a rest home necessary. Lynda still clings to her life, although totally incapacitated, as of this writing.*

My dear old friends,

For we are old friends, aren't we... goodness, it must be 19 years, and in that time
we have all passed some sort of Church Creek Divide, where the waters split on a bit
of schist and flow diversely and come back to Sycamore Canyon, or Partington...and
the sea and we all fly up together in the lovely spindrift. We are not the same people we were at Livermore Ledge, and yet we are.

I deem that the Great Mysterious looks after its wayward ones, for in the whole summer I have had such diversity of employment and entertainment, of panic, boredom and
high excitement, that as the days draw down, it seems to me to have been a magnificent experience. Even in the seemingly small things -- which are the big ones here
-- I have been blessed. I had not had a copy of either Time or Saturday Review until
yours came, and it made such an important change of view, as if after three months I
had discovered a new batch of degrees on the firefinder. From cover to cover have
they been gorged, until I feel as if I were literally eating them all.

Which brings me to the consumption of paper. I measured the water in my cistern this
morning, and found only eleven inches and the layer of lizards, dead froglets and old
rattlesnakes. The man who was here last season managed to wangle a case or two of
beer each triweekly trip, and to keep it cool he hung the bottles, labels and all,
into the cistern. I feel that my innards must be one big life-size papier mache
model of the human gut, and that I shall wake up some morning and find myself broken
out all over with "Burgermeister, Burgermeister, it's a truly fine pale beer."

The evening gossip hour on the radio is filled with speculation. In the San Luis
District, they have a rain pool, each setting a date. The old man on Branch Mountain
has a Farmers Almanac, which he allows has never let him down, and by golly, we'll
have an early winter. The husband of Black Mountain shot a puma the other day and
he's never seen a big cat with so thin a pelt as this one at this time of the year,
and he wouldn't wonder if we didn't have much rain before Christmas. I go along with
my favorite, Ethel on Santa Ynez, whose mountain burned in the Refugio fire and who
stayed by the radio while the flames licked the bottom step and one man was killed
trying to get to her. Ethel says, "Well, I guess it'll rain when it rains."

Have you worked in the Service since the intercom came in? It's exceedingly
interesting to go through a 3 week fire on the sole evidence of the sizzling airborne
dispatching, directing, sometimes inadvertent cursing, torn and weary conversations
from tanker to tanker or dozer to dozer, or ranger to ranger.

"Hey, someone go and pick that man up. He's lying on the road down by Bee Rock. He
fell off his cat."

And hours later, in the middle of the night, over a handy talkie: "Jesus... this
man's dead. I come to git him, and he's dead, I tell you, he's dead."

"Jim, the fire has jumped the river into Paradise. Get the Santa Barbara police.
Have them bring out enough vehicles to evacuate 200 women and children."

"Hey, we got an extra copter here. I dunno who it belongs to."

And a small clear little-girl voice, breaking the sound barrier -- for of course we
were not allowed to breathe over this frequency for 3 weeks except checking in and
out -- and the little girl said, "Is it all right, Bob, if I take the afternoon off
to get my wedding license?"

But in some subtle and some obvious ways, the Service has changed mightily in the
past years; at least in my opinion not for the better. The radio seems to have done
it. Inevitably it hitched up the whole forest into one big unity. Inevitably it put

us on an army basis, with foolish little codes, no single unnecessary syllable ever spoken over the air during business hours and in this district, because of a certain dedication to Duty on the part of Cone Peak, who hovers over our destinies, not more than a few sentences in the evening. If, outside of smoke reports, I must say something to the office, I write it down on paper, time its reading to inside two minutes, hurriedly say my "10-4, Pinyon" and hang up with the sense that I've probably got a black mark on my report card -- which doesn't bother me of itself, but has bothered me because of all its implications of regimentation. By now, I have come to think it only laughable in this framework. I can see them figuring it all out. 10-4, Okay. 10-6, stand by. 10-7, gone to the john. 10-8, back from the john. And in order to save air time, No is Negative (Three times the monosyllable) and Yes is Affirmative, four times. All messages "Brief, impersonal and unemotional." So I go out on the catwalk and bawl poetry at length, most personally and with the utmost emotion.

And I see how this increases misunderstanding, and that the best laid semantics go oft agley.

Just at the moment, the lookout on Cerro Alto is being yanked off station. About an hour ago the San Luis Ranger station called Car 603 and asked him to go up to the lookout as he hadn't checked in in 24 hours, and if the man was sick to bring him down. So, reading interlinearly, as we do, the thing sounds suspicious. Cerro Alto must be a funny guy, has a voice that sounds pretty rocky at times. Half an hour later, the patrolman called from Cerro Alto to say the lookout had gone out for a walk the night before and had just got in -- 11 a.m.! Then the lookout got on the intercom and muttered something, but was apparently bopped in the bean by aforementioned patrolman. And just now, over handy talkie of patrolman, "I'm having a little difficulty here. Shall I stand by at the lookout?" "Use your own judgment. Bring him down anyway." Not too unemotional either. So you see, life can be beautiful, piecing together bits of old parchment for the story of Pinyon Peak.

Shanagolden darling, I have put off speaking of the state of your health. I have from my mother, almost a total inability to believe in illness, a kind of blind spot. So, since I do not find myself in a position to run across the Upper Arroyo Seco, past Indian Valley and down the Partington Ridge trail to mess up your life and house with all love and well-meaning, I shall keep on believing in health and strength and in the irrefrangible spirit that is Shanagolden. It would be impossible to tell you how much I have learned from you in the years, or how much I love you. From the reedy weed of a glamour puss who came to the Log House 20 years ago, some sort of stalk against the elements has risen, and there is much of you in it. So a little rest is indicated, and who in all the world but Harrydick could so suffice to restoration? If there is anything I can do, after this stretch, grab the grapevine and there I'll be.

You have perhaps heard of my various friends trying to walk up this appalling road. The twelve miles from the locked Forest Service gate must have been that Third Day in the evening when God almighty created Earth, a couple of days before he thought up Great Whales. These being, I understand, the youngest mountains in the world, all the Lord had left were some heaps of old schist and sheest and shale, and the last and worst of these are Pinyon Peak. The road to the ridge on the coast is a freeway. I don't think I ever knew what UP meant until the day Jack Curran brought me up here. Lest you have already heard about Hilary's effort, I'll not go off into the details. After dithering about one whole afternoon -- the office had called at 1 p.m. to say that he had already started -- I picked up a white spot far far down the road, moving. So I made up a bed down in the cabin, whipped up a rice ring, and fetched water to wash the corpse. 7 p.m. I am pacing the catwalk with new (51 dollar) bifocals and F.S. binoculars when fire breaks out down in the middle of the road, 3-4 perilous miles away. I report fire in closed area, doubtless one H.A. Belloc, who, being British and presumably sober, would not do an irresponsible civic act. (True, but not believed) Must be a distress fire.  Am instructed to wave flashlight.  Wave flashlight.  One hour of waving flashlight, sizzling intercom, fire going up, down, up, down.  8 p.m. Elmer -- King City dispatcher -- grabs State jeep pickup, State patrolman, drives the 2-hour misery of this wilderness track to pick up criminal.  10 p.m.: "Pinyon -- Car 628.  Have contacted Party and taking him back to King City.  Fire has been put out.  Car 628, signing off for the night."  It was a distress fire.  Hilary was just about dead.  He wrote, three weeks later: "There is this to be said: that whereas you get yourself into the damndest spots, I get myself into the god-damndest fixes....  I hope you said to your bosses, 'He's only a mad Englishman.  I hardly know him.'"

Well, children, this wretched scrawl is one of the end pieces of a long spell o' writin' down things in snatches.  Selfishly, to amuse myself.  What with one sprained ankle, one bad session of food poisoning, one sudden successful leap over a serpent with bells, an earthquake a day, a few exciting fires, some amusing but not diligent reading, a disappearing cat, six foxes, a handsome young forked horn (who has now a-wooing gone, preferring this, I take it, to fig newtons) and a grand total of seven human faces in almost four months, this has been my summer.  Complete solitude is not recommended.  I often think of Mr. Schmidt -- Beth's husband -- and that, even in prison when you're free, you're relatively free.  Difficult unto terror as it has always been for me to cope with human beings -- with the single exception of my mother -- this continuous solitude is too much at last.  Finally, the vast perimeters, so beautiful and exciting at first, close in.  They clutch at your integument like hairshirts in the wind and the catwalk a steel girdle.  I look down at the Mission San Antonio at 5:30 in the morning and see the lights go on and there is a sort of disbelief that even the Brothers, confined in body and chasuble, may speak to visitors, may walk in their gardens at evening.

But I *believe* that all experience is good.  And that never again will I *walk* the earth, speak or listen to my kind, that I do not remember what it's like not to be able to.

To ride down the coast with Eddie, to walk up the Partington road, to set my eyes upon your wonderful, beautiful faces!

All love,
Lynda
10-4, Pinyon

*Men go mad in this line of work (as fire lookout)... women, too, go mad in the solitary confinement of a mountain peak, though not so readily as men, being stronger, more stable creatures, with a lower center of gravity.*

*Edward Abbey, ABBEY'S ROAD*

```
Same ole mountain,
Same old cat,
Same old bag, and
Same old Bat,
Same "No Welcome"
On the mat.        Pinyon Peak, rah, rah, rah...
```

This year, the Spirit of the U. S. Forest Service and the little spirit of one Lynda Sargent are somewhat at odds. Every year the tone of the Service, as the tone of everything else almost, leans farther and farther toward Ike, Franco & Co. Every year they have to "contact" each other, in "conference" and Full uniform, and make up something that binds about the belly button. The really awful thing about it, when you become an active ingredient of it, is that you can see their reason for doing it and they can't -- quite. Of course, the moment communications became contemporary we are done for as to anything like privacy or freedom or initiative. Last year, in the evening, we were allowed a modicum of friendly intercourse over the intercom after office hours. This was a little attenuated during the highest danger weather, which I'm sure we all understood. Certainly in this district we all gladly acquiesced.

For a lone person like myself, after a day of talking exclusively to me, those brief evening chats were charming. You called only one person yourself, and chatted about something that had happened during the day.

"Hello, Marie...is your kitty all right after the rattlesnake bite? My, weren't the clouds lovely at sunset time. Well, good-night...see you tomorrow."

Maudie Yates -- do remember Kurt and Maudie -- called High Mountain in the San Luis District every night at 9 on the dot, and they swapped recipes and dog stores for a few minutes. A 19 year old boy on Cuyama Peak read the illiterate poem he'd written for the day. Just before we shut our radios off for the night, Lorraine from Santa Barbara, an assistant dispatcher -- the only woman with that rank in the Forest -- and one with a beautiful voice, dropped her official role and tone and talked a little about the day. Nearly every night ended with her charming -- "All's quiet in the zone. Good night."

Abuse of a privilege is the commonest event in human experience. But there were so few who did abuse it. It seems to me that a slap on the back of the hand would easily have accomplished discretion. And you two will so easily understand how much it meant, not only to me, but to all. And how important it was.

Now it is over. We may talk 30 seconds. And the result is that no one talks at all. The directive is that we may talk between 8 and 9 for 30 seconds at a time, then a 30 second break, and another 30 second message and then -- nothing. As I say, no one talks at all. During the day we may report a smoke. They have got out a form for that. It's exactly the same old thing, but a special form at great cost to the tax-payer, has been printed for it.

It's like the little boy whose mother asked him why he didn't accept a piece of pie offered by a neighbor, and he said, "Aw, 'tain't the pie, Ma. It's the spirit of the old woman."

Ah, me! No more feeling of one great big happy family.

One incident, and I gotta get windows washed.

In the middle of a baked potato the other evening, my gas went out. A new tank to be installed. I ran downstairs, only to find that I could not budge the nut on the gas line. I know all about the reverse threads and so forth, but the thing had been on all winter and was rusty. I'll not bore you with details, but hard as I tried, tapping a hammer *gently* on the great pipe wrench which must have tightened all the nuts and pipes on the Mighty Mo, I had to give up. When I checked in to Cone Peak that night, I mentioned it, only to ask if he had any suggestions.

Next morning was Sunday. I had a jolly time, getting my breakfast on the wood stove down in the cabin. Toast tastes good made on a rusty piece of hot iron. The dawn was beautiful. I had got up at 5:30 to do it and so had the unaccustomed delight of almost an hour down below, before I wrapped boiled eggs, toast and bacon in a dish-towel and brought it up here to eat. Boo and I danced in the morning and sang together. Only ten days to supply trip and I looked forward to ten mornings out of tower. Chucked the stove full of wood, set the bucket on before I came up, and had all the hot water I could use. 104 degrees in Arroyo Seco that day and cold food -- even cold coffee made with powdered Folgers -- was fine.

Eight o'clock and things started busting. Two patrolmen called the office to ask if they might come up and turn that nut. Elmer said they'd take care of it themselves. After the fiasco about Hilary, I wanted least of anything in the world to put the task on the Service. Called Elmer and told him so, that I was all right...perfectly all right.

Next afternoon at a little after 5 I am just getting out my coffee-can-pottie when I see a space ship coming straight at pot. Button up shorts and get to catwalk just in time to see a funny glass punkin, waving four great arms and wiggling long yellow tail, set neatly down on my new heliport.

Out tumbles Superman. Out steps stylish youth in full panoply of First Lieutenant of U.S. Army, Helicopter Division. Super Hand copes with nut, lifts 90-lb gas tank like baby, screws on. Indicator flies to Full. Three minutes at most. No thank you, no time for coffee. Back into punkin. Round and round go whirling arms...Come Donner...Come Blitzen. Chug from gizzard of punkin. Punkin barely clears foot-high manzanita. Drops a couple of hundred feet into Horse Canyon. Levels off. Exactly seven minutes later, they touched the runway at Hunter Liggett, in time to wash off the grease before chow.

This, I think, may not generally be bruited about -- at least not in print, as what irate citizen would yell bloody murder about taxpayers' money. However, everyone around here knows about it.

I must leave the Cachagua this fall. Nothing left there for me, though I have had *much* out of it, in my own way. So if you hear of anything. A lot of muddy water, and some very crystal clean, has gone under logs and rootlings, since I began to "go out to work." Most important, I've learned not to talk about the people I work for. And I've learned that, it ever being incredibly difficult for me to be with people much, I have to take the measure of submission to the ways of others, without impairing my own so-called integrity. All I ask for, after all, is a pleasant, literate, castrated male of about 70, complete with Thunderbird which he dislikes to drive, small but charming house and maidservant, discreetly affluent, requiring a retiring companion on annual trips abroad, acutely sensible of the sacrifice anyone makes who does a thing besides loaf under a baobab tree, and ready at all times to implement his conviction that a woman should dress with some feeling for taste and elegance. You will note that I haven't mentioned personal remuneration. Given all else, I can handle that.

Or, alternatively, a beat up old ex-professor of the humanities, with a hundred a month, who wants to shack up.

Bye now, darlings...let me have news of your good selves.

And the old and very dear love,
Lynda
July 3

The morning of the twenty-fifth of September, 1957
Love and greetings to dear old friends over yonder at 274 degrees on the back side of the firefinder.

I got up at dawn, and to hell with Sean O'Faolain. Dawn, says he, is a boss-word, not to be used by prose writers. Actually, I rose from my bed at full dark, went pottie in my two-pound coffee can, squinted at the face of the clock to find that it was 5:15, and decided to stay up to see the handsome salmon coloured glow from the Nevada proving grounds. It didn't materialize, or perhaps it was what awakened me; it sometimes does. The big ones are very beautiful, with greenish coronas.

But I watched the dawn, as I often do, and it's as real as a horse. This is a fine place to see it, as I have a 24-mile open stretch between me and the low hills above Priest Valley eastward. If Mr. O'Faolain has a synonym for the few moments when the dark becomes dusk and the first apricot-tinted intimation of light begins to brighten the horizon, I don't want to know it, I don't. Remember his "romantic words"? Dawn, dew, youth, world, adamant, dusk. Dew is a globule of water deposited at the atmospheric dew point. If you wipe out youth, what are you going to do about age? And in one of his own pet stories, in the same issue of Atlantic, he writes, "It was dusk." I'm all gollywoggled about this semantic, which seems to me to do nothing but substitute one boss word for another. Quien sabe! Incidentally, it looks from here as if the Quien Sabe school outside of Hollister must be within that big burn at this moment.

If you want to go in for mind reading, there's money in it.  A fortnight ago, or so,
there was no acceptable reading matter in the library at Pinyon Peak.  I had wearied
of the ponderous tomes I bring up here, and had packed them all away when I went down
on sick leave.  There was the book of cloud forms, which I've long wanted to dig
into, and some small angel, trailing across the Monterey Division of Los Padres, had
absent mindedly dropped the whole sack.  Eastward, I had the high gleaming tufted
cirrus, the mare's tails of old time.  Hunter Liggett, southeast, had a brilliant
display of rippled altocumulus overhead, with an echo of those horrid jelly bombs
that burn out a man's insides, down below.  Over Chews Ridge way, in the aftermath of
a little rain in Monterey, a span of nimbostratus was topped by castellated fractocu-
mulus, shaking out its plumes 6000 feet above Uncle Sam and Ventana Double Cone.  Oh,
I had a fine time.  I even had, directly overhead, a massive lenticular altocumulus,
trying to find its way home.  Well, if I have to watch my dawns and dusks, what a lot
of wonderful words a word lover may snatch out of the "world" of science and everyday
life.  The hills are still lordly and all the foxes are sleek, greedy and much too
fat for their kind, with all the homemade sugar cookies I stir up daily for them.

The mind-reading...I do digress, but no matter.  The evening of the fog day -- or
should I say at 18:15 of that day? -- I sat down to make out my list of supplies.  In
a sorrowful optimism, I headed my wanted list of reading matter "Harpers, Atlantic,
New Yorker, New Republic." It was, I knew, only an arrogant gesture, showing off to
the other lookouts who would hear all, that I would not *prefer* Satevepost, Readers
Digest, Ladies Home Journal, the only ones I could get outside Argosy and True Con-
fessions which even the office knows better than to send.

Supply trip came up, bringing Richard and his little sister from home, and the girl
Pat busts about the earth with, and there were four packages, all of the same size
and shape.  Opening one, hastily to see if it contained business matter, and finding
a bunch of Examiners, I shoved them all under the bed to have as much time as possible for my niece, assuming them all to be either Hearst or Curtis or Luce excretions.

Nor did I glance at them until the next morning with breakfast in bed.  I confess to
a few tears of relief and gratitude at the very sight of the name Ross.  Now I have
apples for my delectation -- everything good is an apple. I wish I didn't feel that
merely saying Thank You is never enough, but you can mind read my gratitude and
pleasure.  (This pore old machine is drunk with fractocumulonimbus, and refuses to
walk a straight line.  I have tried to tighten up screws but the screwdriver here did
duty on the old MightyMo, and is contemptuous.)

The sick leave.  What puerile wereweevils we are in the face of the unknowns.  Coming
up here in June feeling better than for years after a 3 months rest, I woke of a dawn
with a song on my lips and a pain in the region of one kidney.  Day by day, pain
expanded.  In vain did I assure myself that, having been supplied at birth with a
fresh neurosis and/or psychosis for each day of my life, what was a little pain but
another dimension of imagination.  When it struck deep into the "portions of a woman
that appeal to man's depravity" it picked up an added load of ancient and elemental
fear.  So I finally capitulated and went up to Palo Alto to spend a few days with a
distinguished and beloved friend, Russell van Arsdale Lee, M.D.

Who allowed as how my blood count was incomparably good, blood pressure that of a
woman of 30, urine "sweet enough to drink," heart of a pride of lions, and if not
technically a virgin, no real difference.  Only "extensive spinal arthritis," the old

Sargent mania. Favorite Sargent aunt died after 7 years immobile in bed with it. Father suffered agonies in shoulders and back with it, and now denies he ever had it. By prescription, I gathered up a big bottle of brewers yeast and some bufferin, romped back here, and haven't had a real pain since. Yes, my right elbow, but I suspect the old elbow is just disgusted at being bent too often.

Now, if I ever did take any thought for the morrow, I'd have to look forward to the long haul of the Sargent bones. Well, it will go something like this: Some further evening, I shall dress up for a party. I think I'll wear a bluegreen taffeta to match my still bright one-eye, and put a funny paper hat atop my well-blued hair. Ham actress that I am, I shall wait until all the guests have arrived and make an entrance. Young men will salaam, old men kiss my hand. At approximately 11:45 p.m. I shall begin to have the first sinking spell of my life. And as I sink, I shall get madder and madder that I couldn't have lived another ten minutes to watch the 21st century in.

Speaking of my one-eye, I clipped from one of the pics the first season I was here, a coloured photo of my favorite queen in all history, Queen Nefertiti of Egypt, 1300 B.C., whom you probably recall. (Perhaps you do not feel, as I sometimes do, that I was a King of Egypt, and killed off a thousand slaves to build my tomb.) This queen, whose name means The Beautiful has Come, brings to life, for me, the whole span of that marvellous civilization, which is so much more real to me than the Greek. Sidney and I often spent our Sunday afternoons in the Museum of Natural History in New York. If I lost him, he was invariably in the astronomy section, and if he wanted to find me, I was in Egypt. This bust of Queen Nefertiti lay, as you will recall, for centuries in the Nile mud and was recovered, if memory serves, in 1912. Ah, she is very beautiful! Her poise is regal and the artist who made this likeness has achieved such an uplift in her bearing that I have only to look at her to achieve slenderellaizing. Up goes the chin and the rest comes along.

The comfort she gives me now is incalculable. Aside from the partial loss of one ear, the black onyx stone which was her left eye is missing. This in no way diminishes her effectiveness. My right eye has been diagnosed as incipient cataract -- the diagnosis being rather tentative, I have not yet shared this secret with the Forest Service, as my Bates exercises did me so well that Messier said my general vision was much better than last year, and it is. But I shall probably confess this wickedness to Curran this year and be out of this job. If I can still, next season, as I now can, pick up a wee smoke pot at 20 miles without any extra eyes...time tells.

At this moment I am reminded of something very comforting I heard on the radio last night, which you also may have heard; that for these fall months they have shut off the beacon atop the Empire State building because it is deflecting the migrating birds from their courses. Some of the poor little things turn back northwards, but I cannot believe they're so dumb as not to know what they're doing. I am reminded this morning, because, on this cold, bitter September day, a flight of migrating swallows has hit my tower, flying in terror at all the windows, going round and round and round. With my five-months growth of hair, my windstruck skin which looks like nothing but uncured hoghide, an old skirt that Janet gave me years ago half eaten up by ants, I feel and look like the witch of Pinyon Peak, and would like to take to my great broom and shoo them south. Alas, the south gale which rocks the tower this morning, would perhaps make steering difficult and we'd all land in the Klamath fire.

Shucks.  I see that my horde of foxes has got into the refrigerator down below -- the door of which I left ajar as I'm not using it now -- and are merrily consuming the six loaves of bread.  Also, eggshells skitter about in imitation of swallows and I'd best go down and retrieve what I may of the five dozen eggs.  I can easily make biscuits, but all the eggs I've deposited have had inedible yolks.

Much love to you both, and it will be a glad day a few weeks from now, when I can drop in on Partington Ridge.  The time has arrived when I don't know that I would trust my neck-throttling hands if one of those frail young females who has never yet been out of sight and sound of the butt and belly of homo sapiens, came up to me with clasped hands, gazed awestruck into my face, and exclaimed in high C, "Oh, how I would *looove* it...alone...all alone on Parnassus...alone with the gods."

Lynda

The seventh day of October ... which seemed a millenium away in June.

Oh, my dear friends, what a morning! What a week! What a place!

And you, of all my friends, will know what the morning is like.  A beautiful Blake, all chiaroscuro and then rainbows.  Mighty six thousand foot high rivers and little rills of fog, flowing and dancing and muddling everywhere.  Only old Junipero Serra and I have had the wonderful privilege of seeing it all.  Two pots of gold rest in a bush on the south flying buttress of Pinyon, and two on the crag north where the golden tailed hawks nest in June.  Almost a complete hoop, and I feel that I could take the tall dead yucca I brought in for the seed pods and the lovely ivory spikes and roll it off into Horse Canyon.  Boo and I have been racing and cavorting with the dews, singing paeans and saying poesy.

Thursday noon I was puddling away at a lemon souffle, with corn meal mush bubbling for lunch, and the world lighted up with a glorious flash from a black cloud coming straight at Pinyon from Hollister, northeast.  Before I could lay down the eggbeater, another came from the Carmel Valley, northeast.

Now for thirty-seven years of my life I lived in thunderstorm country. Up the valley of the Contoocook River below us came the mammoth bronze-hearted castellated thunder-heads, and down the course of Ami Brook westward came some more, and they met in the village of Henniker, or on the hill farms around us, and crashed and bellowed. My mother, whose foolish mother had been frightened out of her poor wits and had always taken to her feather bed, was resolved that her children would never be so slavish to fear. She would take us by her trembling hands and lead us out into it, and in a voice breaking with terror, exclaim, "Isn't it lovely! See that forked lightning. How beautiful!" Balls of fire would run down the telephone pole across the road. If we could count to three between strike and clap, we deemed ourselves safe, but some-times we couldn't. We were terrified, but not afraid. The only time it came too close, one of Mother's purebred Suffolk Punch mares, who hadn't read the lookout instructions, and had taken refuge under a lone tree in the field, came galloping up to the dooryard with a head four times the size of a horse head and had to be shot. One memorable night, a great barn across the valley suddenly went up in flames, and we could hear the cattle and horses and hogs screaming. But we were never afraid.

I put the eggbeater into cold water and called Elmer and told him that he had just been struck by lightning. He said he knew it, and forthwith all his communication went out. With an old glove on my right hand I disconnected both radio antennae, closed all the windows, turned off the oil stove and admitted the petrified cat. I got a notepad and a fistful of sharp pencils and my bowl of mush and milk and climbed up on the wobbly glass heeled stool and began to record. She came and sat on top of the tower. For half the compass, the big red bolts jabbed into the canyons around. I ran around like a decapitated biddy, taking readings, scribbling shorthand. Twice the tower was struck, but it didn't come down the stovepipe, only ran down the lightning rods seven feet from my nose.

When she veered off west and trailed exhausted out over Big Sur, I gave my readings to Chews Ridge to phone into King City, and wiped the sweat from all my interstices, and set myself to watch these Coulter pines in Horse Canyon. It had been terribly exciting, just wonderful, and the reaction set in by evening.

At six o'clock Elmer was back on the air and he called and complimented me, and I hung my head and muttered "Thank you. 10-4 Pinyon." I was as embarrassed as a third grader who has been cited before the whole class for an A in arithmetic. Mostly, I was sorry for all these California lookouts who get so scared they hide and shudder.

I knew that there would be no sleep for me that night, and at 7:30 I sat down to write to Ezra. The wind bellowed three gales at once and all of a sudden I felt so very remote, so very lonely, so utterly out of the world. I wrote: "If I believed in the answer to prayer, I'd pray to have just one human face to talk to tonight."

I went out on the catwalk at the end of the sentence and there was a blaze at the foot of Horse, and a gale coming my way. Chalome reported it and so did I. You know what happened then. Wheels began to roll. The air sizzled. I froze to the catwalk rail.

At a little before nine, Elmer called to say that Bob Nelson and the Arroyo Seco crew were on their way up, in case the fire came this far. They would arrive about mid-night. I busied myself making up beds down in the cabin, lugging up buckets of water, readying the eight-cup coffee pot, mixing biscuits. I put together a few things in a small suitcase and got the cat's box up here.

By ten o'clock the fire, only a small blaze, had been controlled.  At twelve I saw the lights of the International come up Reliz Canyon and over the ridges.  Elmer called to say that he was going to bed.  Elmer is a sleeper; he hates to be roused from his good slumbers.  At one o'clock Bob called from his handie talkie to say that he had run the truck off the road, and please call Elmer and ask him what to do. "Tell 'em to walk up," said Elmer grumpily, and went back to bed.

One of the clock, and flashlights appeared over Bear Mountain at my feet.  I put the coffee pot on.  Two thirty, and nine men climbed my stairs.  I should pray for pence; coffers would run over.  Four a.m. and they all went to bed but me, and I got ready for the new day.  Elmer got Butch with the power wagon, and Alvin Brazil and Joe Perry to come and get the truck on the road.  They took all day, and I had all the talk I needed for centuries.  The hill was littered with Mexican boys.  Midafternoon, the Big Sur crew came and hauled them all down the hill.  Solitude and silence were suddenly celestial.  I half dread the supply trip this week, which will replace the bacon and eggs and coffee and beans.

Now I am praying that this thing clears up, for we have had a little over an inch of rain and I don't want to go down until there are a few more of those long green pieces of cardboard stashed down in the office for me.

And now I'd better tackle this heap of mail, catch up on my log, eat my corn meal mush and wash out some nylons.  Keep well, Shanagolden...well and busy and happy, both of you. And though I do not permit much thinking on the subject yet, the day I can slog up the road from the mail stage and eat corn meal mush with you will be that bright and heavenly day for me.  It's been a strange summer, with some bootstrapping, but the vertebrae seem to be intact, and what with cutting down to three fags a day and not a drop of the juice of the grain, I feel better than for years.  Perhaps henceforth the United States Forest Service can squeak along without me, but at the moment life seems full of fascinating things for a sixty-year old freshman to gape at, and the same to you and much love,

Lynda

The young Mexicans called out as they rolled down the road, "Goodbye Mother."

*Alone, we are close to nothing. In prolonged solitude, as I've discovered, we come very close to nothingness. Too close for comfort.*

*Through the art of language, most inevitable of the arts, -- for what is more basic to our humanity than language? -- we communicate with others what would be intolerable to bear alone.*

*Edward Abbey, ABBEY'S ROAD*

*"I'm not just a nice little old lady. I have a nose for getting into all kinds of things,"
says Virginia Louise Swanson, who at one time held twenty-two mining claims in the
Santa Lucias.*

# A Woman Miner in the Santa Lucias

### by Judith Goodman

Adventure was the lure that drew Virginia Louise Swanson to the remote wilderness of the Los Burros Mining District, deep in the inaccessible heart of the Santa Lucia Mountains. These steep, rocky ridges and thickly wooded canyons of the "South coast" had witnessed a two hundred year procession of determined men following tales of gold for the taking; first the Spaniards seeking the hidden cave full of gold pebbles of Indian legend, later Mexicans with pick and shovel, and since the Gold Rush an ebb and flow of mining activity that peaked toward the end of the century. Fortunes were made and lost in Los Burros.

By 1950, when Virginia found her way to the district, Los Burros was deserted by all but a few old-timers living on their claims. The easy pickings were gone. The time was ripe for scams, as the Highway and the new Forestry roads enticed "greenhorn" miners into the area seeking gold and adventure.

"I was just a newcomer, you know," says Virginia, "just a patsy." When an old-timer offered to sell her a claim, she couldn't resist. For this fifty year old lover of the outdoors, raised on a rugged Cascade Mountain homestead, used to the outdoor life, and a rockhound to boot, a twenty acre mining claim was just the thing to balance out her nine-to-five job as a test chemist for Pet Milk Company in Salinas. She bought Valle de Oro.

For six months, on weekends and vacations, driving the hundred miles of treacherous Highway One, Virginia labored to set up a base camp. From her car on Gold Ridge she hauled supplies down a near vertical hill to the creek, then back up the other slope to her camp on Volcano Ridge. In her book *Night Side of Gold* she describes the operation:

> Up at my car, I unloaded more supplies, piled a stack on a three foot platform normally used to stack canned goods for shipment. These I used for sleds which I could pull down the steep hill to the creek, then up the easier climb...to the steep knoll where my permanent camp would be established. I wound one end of my hauling rope around my waist, inched my crude sled along. By sundown, everything was up to my knoll. My last bottle of orange soda and my last ounce of strength gave out about the same time.

In six months she had a one-room cabin with floor, roof, walls, two windows and a door -- "all nailed piecemeal by whoever I could inveigle into a couple hours work."

At the end of six months of exhausting labor, the oldtimer informed her with regret that he had sold her the wrong claim -- "Pa's old claim, which I couldn't keep, but not to worry, he had a better claim, just right for me -- for just a little more money."

Virginia may have been a "greenhorn" but she was a quick learner. "They had the quaint old outdoor custom of selling you a mining claim and getting your money. I got sucked in on that. Except, I un-sucked. When I realized what had been done, I wouldn't give up."

She learned how to acquire mining claims legally. She bought a D-2 (a small bulldozer) and an old jeep. Before she was through in Los Burros, Virginia was owner or partner in twenty-two claims, and had tramped over many miles of rugged country, measuring the boundaries with crochet thread -- "a 1500 foot spool for side lines, a 600 foot spool marked each end line. A nifty way to straighten a line across gullies and ridges."

*Soon I acquired a better cabin close to the road on Gold Ridge. I leased a chromite mine; with crew and friends we mined and hauled the required pay-load with my jeep; struggling steep-out of a bowl of serpentine -- half the load boxed on the front bumper to prevent tipping over backward. The ore was picked up at a loading ramp down on the highway by truck and hauled to the government depot in Grant's Pass, Oregon.*

*Enroute several tons disappeared at night -- enough to enrich a rejected load of poor quality ore.... No way could such theft be proven, so forget it.*

*The problem, in one word, was resentment. There was no such thing as a woman miner -- only a woman -- and fair game to be victimized in any way possible.*

In nine years of killing effort, the chromite venture was Virginia's only successful attempt at mining. She was heckled and harrassed, bullied and cheated and tricked. Guns were fired over her head while she was camping -- all in hopes of intimidating her and driving her out. As Virginia put it, "I didn't drive worth a damn." But she never found time to mine for gold.

In 1962 while recovering from a severe acid burn, Virginia received an unwelcome summons. As required by new mining laws, she must post $250 for each of her twenty-two claims and appear in court to prove that production warranted "a prudent man" continuing to work the claims. Virginia -- a prudent woman -- knew it was time to give up in Los Burros. To this day she considers her leaving a narrow escape. "So help me, if I'd stayed any longer I would have killed somebody."

Frustrated every way she turned, why did Virginia stick it out for almost a decade? Not the gold, but the mysteries of the land itself, brought her back, time after time, in an attempt to understand the unseen forces at work there. From the beginning, she had strange encounters, unexplained experiences, intriguing to Virginia, a life-long believer in the occult.

*My first encounter with monster-creatures moving around in the dark awakened me from an exhausted sleep by an over-powering stench. I heard three heavy creatures approach and surround my cot -- grunting; wild pigs, I supposed, until I was picked up, cot and all -- and dropped when I screamed.*

*My second encounter occurred atop my camp mound, also at night. A strange howl changing to a scream from a serpentine ridge above was answered by another across the canyon. Within minutes, "things" with glowing eyes circled my mound, screaming; I stayed up all night to keep my campfire burning.*

*That date -- 1952 -- I had never heard of Bigfoot -- only the Abominable Snowman in some vague and distant place.*

Old-timers were generous with spooky tales of werewolves, murders and ghosts. A reputable researcher convinced her that the Indian midden on her Valle de Oro claim had been a ceremonial gathering place for ancient tribes. She sensed their presence. In the high country she encountered a mother wolf nursing her cubs and heard a voice reassure her that it was just a little animal protecting its young. She arranged to have a lion-hunter seek the animal that was making the unearthly night howling, and the trained dogs were terrified and refused to follow the tracks. She experienced a vision of "a long row of mountain men lined up along the high bank, looking down at me. All wore dark jackets and slouch hats of another era -- their faces hidden behind beards. I had seen them clearly; in seconds they were gone. I have no explanation."

*Make no mistake about it, there is something uncanny about that Coast Range... certain areas of the mountains conceal dark secrets... evil powers; those who must travel the highway that threads the cliffs*

*above the coast should pass quickly
lest harm befall...*

With the help of six metaphysically inclined friends, Virginia attempted to exorcize the evil spirits that haunted her claim.

> *(We) ...donned our white robes -- fastened our candles in the glass holders, each a different color. The Chanting One traced the outline of a six pointed star on the meadow. Each of us placed our cushion at one of the points, lit our candles, sat down and waited in silence. Immediately, we were aware of an invisible force like a thread of electric power encircling us. Softly, the Chanting One began her invocation.... Then the chant, beautiful beyond description. Whatever the language, the music of it poured forth from the depths of the soul, a fountain of color-tone, lifting each of us for a brief moment in time to a realm beyond human knowledge. Such a moment of transcendental beauty... could such a moment endure, we would know the Way.*

Los Burros Mining District had never seen the likes of this before.

It was not until several years after she left Los Burros that Virginia began to suspect that she had been witness to several appearances of the legendary man-ape, Bigfoot. Through research and contact with other seekers after unpopular truth, she has been tracing Bigfoot appearances and has developed her own theories about what it is, where it comes from and why it lingers in the haunts of men. At the spry and alert age of eighty-two, Virginia now tramps the high desert around Julian, California, seeking to communicate with the elusive beast. She and two other women have joined forces in a new approach to making contact with Bigfoot.

> *Every expedition that's made up of men go with traps and guns and they want to capture it. We figure this way. The feminine approach of compassion, of sympathy in trying to reach through kindness and an offer of help -- that's the attitude I'm working on.*

Virginia's decade in Los Burros was only one chapter in a full and varied life. Bigfoot is only one of the mysteries that intrigue her.

> *There are things in this world we have not begun to discover. I want to find out what all great men have wanted to know. Why are we here and what is my role in the scheme of things? Until I die, I will continue to search.*

*Photos courtesy of Virginia Swanson*

*Change is a constant here in Big Sur, as everywhere else in the world. Since the writing of this interview with Rosa Nash, she and Bob have decided to seek a period of solitude in their lives. Rosa is now living at the Immaculate Heart Hermitage in Big Sur, while Bob remains on Partington Ridge.*

# An Interview with Rosa Nash

## by Kristin Trotter

I parked down on Partington Ridge Road and walked up through the redwood trees and out onto the sunny hillside where Bob and Rosa Nash make their home. The setting was peaceful -- even the dog that rushed out to greet me did not bark, but licked my hand and led me through the gate and up the path to the studio.

Inside, a bed covered with sleeping cats, a wall of etchings, drawings and icons, and a shelf of books on art, mathematics, religion and philosophy. On the desk was Bob's latest project -- a course in Mandarin Chinese.

We settled down beside the wood stove and Rosa began to talk. Everything about her was calm. She spoke slowly and chose her words carefully.

I was raised in Los Angeles, the second oldest of eight children. Since my early teens there have been three dominant realizations that have stayed with me to this day: the deep conviction of how quickly life goes; the desire to seek God; and the preference for an "un-ordinary" life, one stripped of "things." Although I dated heavily in my youth, I kept feeling that God wanted me to serve Him in a special way and so at 22 I entered the convent. I taught high school English for 15 years, later became a school principal, and finally, a school supervisor.

In the early 1960's the Immaculate Heart community to which I belonged bought Louisa Jenkins' house on Partington Ridge in Big Sur, and in 1965 another nun and I went there for a week's rest. I had never heard of Big Sur before then. When we arrived at the house, my companion said nervously, "Rosa, I don't see any other houses. It's all just wilderness." When I stepped out of the car and looked around at all this natural beauty I exclaimed, "I belong here." I had never felt like this before. Besides, nuns never said such things; you simply went wherever you were called.

Shortly after we arrived, there was a knock at the door and there stood Bob, his hair down to his shoulders, wearing a blue jean jacket, pants and heavy work boots. He very courteously introduced himself: he was the caretaker -- did we need firewood or anything? My friend was still nervous, but I thought "How nice, here's someone to talk to." We talked for hours, mostly about education. He was intelligent, enjoyable company. Later, we invited him for dinner several times.

One day that week he asked us up to see where he lived, so the two of us hitched us our navy blue skirts and followed him up the dirt pathway. All he had to protect his mattress and few belongings was a red wooden structure; everything else was outside. In front of the shelter was a slab of redwood and on it was a vase with a single daffodil, a book on poetry, and a copy of the daily New York Times. The absolute simplicity of his life was a revelation.

And so began an evolution. After we went back to Los Angeles, I came back to the Jenkins' house maybe once or twice a year for the next three years. Bob and I began a precious correspondence. In that interim there were great changes in my life. I had my first heart operation to correct a valve damaged by rheumatic fever. This surgery devastated me physically and emotionally. Radical things went wrong in the surgery. I was dying three times. It took me a year to regain even moderate health.

I've had two other heart operations to replace my mitral valve with a valve taken from a pig. As the porcine valve lasts only 8 to 10 years, I must look forward to surgery every decade. Facing and experiencing these surgeries is the most difficult thing I've ever had to do. Such violence to the body, such violence to the person. I feel myself on an altar of sacrifice -- holding myself together, concentrating all my energies on this one act; trying to pass through the experience and transcend it. It must be done and I must survive.

In 1968 I came to live in Big Sur. Some months before, I accepted the fact that I was in love with Bob. He was the most reverent person I had ever known, the most truly religious. I applied to Rome for a dispensation from my vows. Three weeks later I received it, and in September, 1968, Bob and I were married and took up life in Big Sur.

We started out in his camp on a flat 1200 feet above the ocean, with a view both north and south. All we had was a mattress and a VW Bug. Soon we built a winterized tent. A few weeks later, before winter set in, we were invited to caretake the Phelps house, and later Maude Oakes place. Caretaking has been our way of life. In 1973, we moved to Sedona, Arizona, to caretake the Chapel of the Holy Cross. We loved the country there, but we belong in Big Sur, so after a year and a half, we returned to Partington Ridge.

We've had various jobs in Big Sur. Bob, a jack-of-all-trades, did odd jobs, and I tutored. We both worked at the Phoenix Shop at Nepenthe. Later we helped care for Nicholas Roosevelt. One day I asked our good friends the Gagnons, who are successful ceramicists, if I might help them whenever they had a rush order. The result was that Bob and I took up pottery -- making ceramic plaques. That's how we make our living now.

I like the simplicity of life in Big Sur. For me, this coast is a healing environment. Coming through my first heart surgery I kept "seeing" the incredible forests in Big Sur, even individual trees, my favorite aspect of nature. Such an environment nourishes my body and spirit. It heals me. Yes, I am sometimes afraid when I think of my remoteness from doctors. During the disastrous winter of 1983, when we people of Partington Ridge were trapped between slides for three months, I was convalescing from my third surgery. The experience has confirmed my belief that my only way is to rest in God's hands -- there is no other way. He holds my life in his hands.

When I am troubled, anxious, afraid, I go outside and contemplate what is before me, the great basic fidelity of nature. Spring does return, the sun does bless us again. These trees have lived my life length again and again. There is stability here, a rhythmic life. I regain my perspective. There's a marvelous Chippewa Indian saying that illustrates the perspective that Nature can give us:

> Sometimes I go about pitying myself when all the time I am being carried by great winds across the sky.

Big Sur has enabled me to grow into a deeper awareness and understanding of animals, both wild and domestic. I never cease to wonder at the complex and loving personalities in our cats and dogs. When they are respected, not dominated, they reveal themselves to us. And it is a marvelous revelation. The "reverence for life" philosophy of Albert Schweitzer, one of my most favorite men, if taken seriously, could transform the whole world, I believe. Living in harmony with all of nature can heal the fragmentation that seems so prevalent today. We become more whole when we respond to the living creatures who also have a place in this cosmic design.

I reflect -- on this mountain -- on life, and how it reveals me to myself if I allow it, if I keep an attentive and open heart. My life experiences have helped me to see more clearly, to love more honestly, to let go of my facades, so that I finally may come to know who I am. I believe we find ourselves when we find God in our own Center.

The Camoldolese Hermitage, south of Lucia, is a special place for me. Stepping out of my daily life of work, relationships, involvements, distractions, to simply be, to wait and listen in that simple retreat room, is an experience I try to allow myself every few months. I love those first few moments just after I've arrived when I've put away simple belongings and stand looking out of the window at the private garden and out to the ocean and say, "Well, Rosa, what's it all about?" For me this retreat experience helps me to regain my perspective before I return to my precious life on the ridge with Bob. In a close relationship of two solitudes it's important to have quiet separate times. Rilke has a fine passage on this close but separate relationship:

> Once the realization is accepted that even between the closest human beings infinite distances continue to exist, a wonderful living side by side can grow up, if they succeed in loving the distance between them which makes it possible for each to see the other whole against the sky.

Some of my nun friends say to me, "Rosa, how can you live up there on that mountain top when there is so much injustice and poverty in the world? There is so much to be done." But you see, I've done all that. I did it for 23 years. In Oriental philosophy life is divided into three parts. First, you study and become educated, then you have your family and lead a life of active involvement, and finally, your life enters the stage where you simplify all things and become contemplative. You naturally move apart from others. There is wisdom in this. Walter de la Mare speaks of life's progress as a "gradual undressing." My life in Big Sur is just that; as someone else put it, an "unpetalling of the flower."

# Four Nudes

## by Eve Miller Ross

Eve Ross (1924--1965) was a woman of many talents. Born Evelyn McClure in Minnesota, the daughter of a theatrical producer, raised in Berkeley, California, she was a top-flight endurance swimmer, spoke five languages, wrote a thesis on Ibsen, and under the stage name of Kevin McClure acted in radio serials and toured the country playing a supporting role in Ibsen's "The Doll House."

Early an admirer of Henry Miller's writing, she came to Big Sur to visit him, and stayed to marry him and to care for his children. As Eve Miller she lived on Partington Ridge during the golden years of that neighborhood when a closely-knit community of writers, artists and kindred souls lived a busy creative and social life. Eve freely gave of herself, taking an active part in the annual Big Sur Revue, especially inspiring the young girls, to whom she brought a sense of glamour and exotic beauty.

In the sixties, she and Henry Miller divorced and she married their next-door neighbor, Harry Dick Ross, an artist and wood sculptor. In his studio, Eve focused on drawing and painting, studying with Helen Colby, Ephraim Doner and others.

Eve died in her sleep one night in 1965, while still at the height of her powers. Among the many friends who felt the great loss was Jory Hopkins, then a young Big Sur girl, who writes of her memories of Eve:

> I remember Eve's hands. She made wonderful things with her hands, gave us love with her hands. There was a beautiful papier mache egg for Easter all colorful that hung from the ceiling, full of little eggs. For all of our theater productions at the Grange she would fit the costumes, inserting little pins, making little tucks. Putting on our make-up she transformed the sweating children into strange princesses, noble kings and butterflies. I would look at myself in the mirror before going onstage and be quite magically different. Eve had long fingers yellow with cigarette smoke and they trembled so it was difficult to see how she put on the make-up so finely. There were some things I didn't understand about Eve.

82

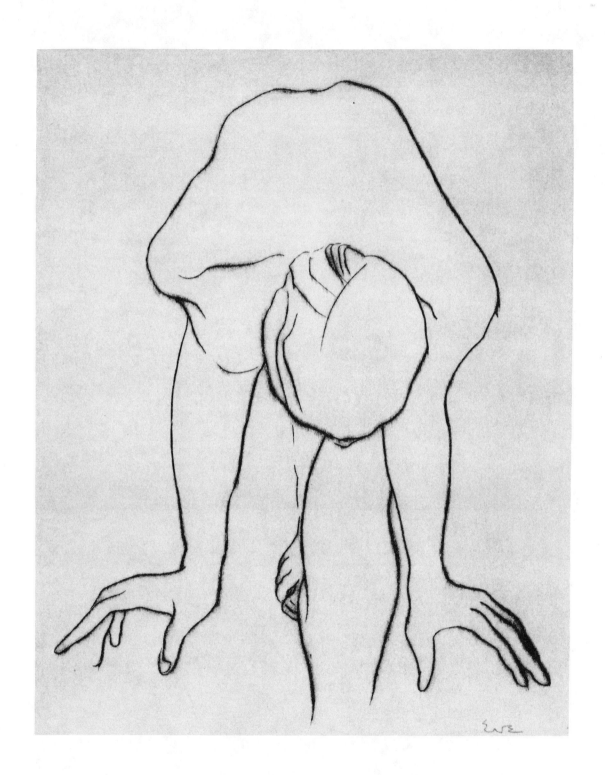

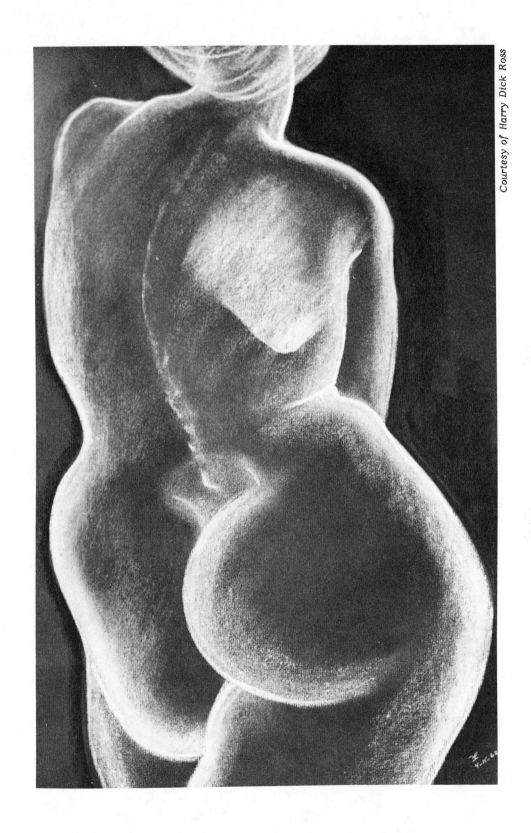

Courtesy of Harry Dick Ross

85

*After twenty-five years of commuting to work from Partington Ridge to Monterey, Theodora Crowley has recently retired to enjoy full-time life on a Big Sur ridge.*

# Home Permanent, Big Sur Style

### by Theodora Crowley

I live in two worlds, two separate life styles in the same time span. My chosen home is perched on a remote mountain top on the edge of the Pacific, with a panoramic view of the Santa Lucia Mountains to the east, the beautiful coastline of Big Sur north and south. I am surrounded by everything I love best, my large assortment of pets (fur, feather and fin), flowers and wall-to-wall books.

The other world I enter five days a week by necessity, commuting to an office with people, computers, stress -- all the components of a "civilized" environment. I do my best with the daily readjustment of my two lives. I wear shoes and proper, if not stylish, garb to the office. As my commute is difficult and time-consuming, an average of 2 1/2 hours a day on Highway One, there just isn't enough time for an elaborate "toilette" before work. I shower and shampoo, get dressed and drive off. My hair gets "blow dried" en route. In good weather, it's dry enough to run a brush through during the straight stretch of highway along Molera and Point Sur. In winter I can usually manage to comb it during the two or three traffic lights in town. Needless to say, this rather casual treatment leaves much to be desired.

My oldest daughter, an elegant cosmopolitan career girl, will try again, on her yearly visit to the "sticks," to persuade her mother that a middle-aged woman with a generous sprinkling of gray, has no business running around with long straight hair. It is simply not becoming!

I survey the heads of my colleagues at the office. Young and old, most seem to have lately sprouted generous curls. How would I look in curls? I might "blend in" better, it might soften my aging face, above all, it might appease my daughter whose visit is imminent. I approach a co-worker with a pleasing amount of waves upon her head and ask, "I like your hair-do. Is it a permanent?"

"Yes, I had it done a couple weeks ago by Mr. X of Cannery Row. I am quite pleased with his work."

"How much did he charge?"

"Fifty dollars. It was a special. Usually it's about sixty-five dollars with tip."

I am deeply shocked. Good grief, that's the equivalent of a bale of hay for the baby llama, fifty pounds of dog and cat food, a sack of chicken feed, some sunflower seeds for the parrots and even a papaya for my cockatoo! No way, not worth fifty dollars for curls.

Around the office coffee machine I sample more heads and opinions. Yes, there are other options. One can go to a beauty school where students do the job cheaper, but much too time consuming for

me. Then there is the do-it-yourself home permanent. On sale at Long's Drug Store for $4.95 plus tax with free curlers thrown in. Voila! That makes more budget sense. I'll do it on my next day off.

The day arrives, a beautiful sunny summer day, if somewhat on the hot side. I do my morning chores, feed all my critters, clean cages, water my flowers. Then I assemble the paraphernalia suggested in the instructions and set to work to better my image. I wash my hair and somewhat clumsily install the curlers in my permanent solution-soaked tresses. The back of the head is a real struggle. I am overjoyed to read in the instruction book: "For the next 60 minutes sit back and relax and let the lotion do its work." This is the part I'm most proficient in.

I concoct my favorite summer drink, Fresca with orange juice and a wee dash of rum. Next I select a mystery from my stack of library books and place myself in a comfortable garden chair under the shade of a tree. For forty-five minutes I am in bliss, clad only in sunglasses and curlers surrounded by beauty and peace. With fifteen minutes left, I decide to replenish my drink with ice cubes. The tray needs refilling; I turn the faucet. Nothing but air hissing at me. No water! My bliss becomes horror. I have only thirteen minutes left before I must rinse the solution out of my hair or risk frizz, or even total destruction of my crowning glory.

Our water source is a year-round mountain creek which travels by gravity flow through a plastic pipe. Perhaps the metal screen filter, a steep 300 feet up the hill, is clogged. I run to the toolshed for a pipe wrench, then up the slope. Rusted shut, I can't budge it. Back down the hill in a frenzy of speed, to get the WD40. Back up the hill, I spray and strain and twist, finally get it open -- it's empty. There is simply no water coming down the mountain. Seven minutes left! Rushing to the phone I call the neighbor nearest the water in-take.

"Kate, do you have water?"

"No, I don't have any either. I don't know what the problem is, maybe a tree fell on the line. The men are doing a town trip today, I'll tell them to check it out when they get back."

I have but four minutes left. Visions of me in an Afro drift through my mind. What if all my hair breaks off at the roots? I could wear a turban, or go bald, wear white flowing robes with beads and tassels, venture out into the "viewshed" and give the tourists an extra treat.

I am sitting by the empty water line, in despair, when my pygmy goat arrives to entertain me with leaps and joyful jumps. The hour is up, my time has run out. The goat -- suddenly, inspiration hits. Only two hours ago I filled the goats' water bucket. I run to the goathouse. The bucket is over half full. Kneeling down, I stick my head in, swishing back and forth and up and down. Tumbleweed, my Angora goat, trots over for a drink, sniffs the water and retreats in disgust.

Well, immediate disaster has been averted. Next step is to put neutralizing solution on hair, leave on twenty minutes, then rinse with clear water. After applying the stuff, I dress in a large towel and hike down the mountain. Twenty minutes later my head is in the bucket of my downwind neighbors who thoughtfully keeps water under the shade of an oak for their three dogs. Home again, curlers removed, I emerge with moderate curls.

Next day at the office:

"Oh, you had your hair done. It looks nice."

"Thank you, it's only a home permanent."

"Really, did you do it all by yourself?"

"Yes -- well, sort of -- except the goats and dogs sure helped."

Strange look, shoulders shrug, well -- weird, -- what do you expect -- she's from Big Sur.

*Born and raised here, this grand daughter of the pioneer Pfeiffer family, Esther (Mrs. Hans) Ewoldsen, knows more about the history and natural history of the coast than anyone else in Big Sur. She also knows that hard work and a positive attitude are the twin secrets of a satisfactory life here. In her column, "The Farmer's Wife" which has appeared monthly in THE ROUND-UP for many years, she provides a glimpse of the practical, everyday life in the calendar year of a Big Sur woman.*

Pat Addleman

*Esther Ewoldsen shares the pioneer craft of sweet grass basketry with Beverly Newell.*

# *The Farmer's Wife*

## *by Esther Ewoldsen*

### JANUARY (1971)

If these rains continue, I'll have to order different types of seeds and bulbs for the garden -- like watercress, watermelon and water chestnuts in the vegetable section and water lilies and water hyacinths in the flower area. I think we have reached or passed some sort of record with over 20 inches of rain before Christmas. It has made the grass grow beautifully on the hills and in my garden too. Each time I was ready to hoe the grass along the paths another storm was predicted, and it arrived! So the grass is still growing.

About half of the orchard is pruned and the rest shouldn't take too long when I get back to it. After doing the trees, the roses will seem like play. The first seed catalogues are arriving so it is time to make out my seed order and then get the seeds planted for later transplanting when gardening time comes around. The storms pretty well ruined my nemesias this year but the stocks are hardier and survived winds and rains and will begin to bloom when the weather dries out and warms up a bit.

## FEBRUARY (1972)

Christopher's duckling is almost fully grown now and turned out to be a lady duck. She is really funny. When she is with the children she follows them about, swims in the tub they have for her, nibbles grass and the potted plants by their house and sits quietly resting. When the children are out of sight, she gets restless until she finds a "people" again; then she sits down and sort of dozes. She's the best flytrap you ever saw -- sneaks up on the unsuspecting insect and flick! Out goes that long neck and the fly is gone. Each time she is returned to the chicken yard, she has a long tale to tell the stay-at-homes with all sorts of soft quackings and head bobbing. The chickens stand around as though they understood her story. She goes with the chickens into the orchard and hunts insects right along with them. She easily learned to climb the ladder with the young chickens and goes up to the roosting level each evening with them. She doesn't sit on the roost but has a preferred corner near the top of the ladder.

Snow peas (edible podded) are blooming so we'll soon have a taste of these again. Turnips are about ready to use, and mustard too. The Chinese cabbage, and regular cabbage and cauliflower are coming along fine. These were planted in mid September. We have a few new potatoes too, from a late planting.

The rest of the garden is cleaned up and the boss Rototilled it the other day to kill grass and weeds that were getting a start. Then I cleaned up the paths so that part of the garden looks pretty neat. The orchard is pruned and trimmings disposed of; blackberries also are pruned and tied up. They had the first of the three necessary sprayings as have the peaches. Next job is pruning the roses, I guess. One climber on an old arbor is going to need a real haircut so I can get at the arbor itself and rebuild it. The wind of that Christmas time storm was too much for the old structure. Another extra job.

Time to plant seed of cabbage type plants and flowers for transplanting later. Tomatoes and peppers can be started early next month if not late this. I feel that I may get time this spring to renovate my rock garden -- at least I'm hoping to do so. It has been many years since I planted it and it needs a good working over. Paper white narcissus and other small flowered ones are blooming, and the daffodils are sending up fat leaves, early types should soon be putting up bud stems. When the daffodils bloom, it is really spring. Violets and winter flowering iris have been blooming for more than a month, buds on the almond tree are swelling and so are those on the early plum.

Good gardening to you too.

## MARCH (1982)

Some early wildflowers are beginning to bloom -- iris, zygadenes, Solomon seal and some ceanothus. I don't know if there will be a good display of annual wildflowers this year. Some times when the grass gets an early start it grows so rampantly that the annuals (poppies, lupines, etc.) -- get crowded out or seem to be lost in the depth of the grasses. Since cattle no longer graze everywhere many of the areas that used to be masses of butter cups, cream

90

cups, baby blue eyes, annual lupines and yellow pansies are now completely taken over by coyote brush, lizard tail, old man, sage, bush lupines, and ceanothus. There is a faint green on the alders by the River which will soon be leaves.

We were up on Pfeiffer Ridge recently and I enjoyed seeing the flowers blooming there. That is a sort of vegetation island, having plants that are not commonly found elsewhere around here. There was manzanita in bloom with its clean foliage and clusters of pale pink bells, quinine bush with long silvery tassels of intricately formed flowers, tree poppies had a few golden blooms and bright Indian warriors stood boldly by the roadside.

The other morning when I fed the chickens I noticed that the outlet of one of the water basins was plugged. So I started to open the small gate to that compartment of the chicken yard to find that I couldn't open it because soil had accumulated in front. A close look disclosed that the gate and the threshold board needed repair. Hoping not to have to make too many trips for materials, I loaded some boards and tools into the wheelbarrow. I had tape, hammer, saw, wrecking bar, pliers, screwdriver, small shovel, assorted nails, my can of unassorted screws. At the chicken yard, the first thing was to remove the gate by taking the screws from the hinges. Then I measured the 2x3 I had selected as a threshhold and sawed it to length only to find it had too much sap wood to last for any length of time at ground level. So back to the lumber pile for a better piece. This I measured, sawed, fitted and nailed into place. Then I put the gate onto supports so I could work on it. Since my new threshhold was considerably thicker than the old one, I had to shorten the gate itself. Removed the rotted bottom board and sawed the side boards to the desired size, but had to return to the lumber supply for a good new bottom board. This in turn was sawed and nailed on the gate. The wire on the gate needed restapling so I had to go to the house for staples. In stretching the wire some of it was so rusted that it had to be replaced, another trip to the supply yard for more chicken wire. At last the gate seemed finished but the hinges needed to be hammered and straightened which wasn't hard to do. It took some sawing of ends here and there to fit the gate into the opening, then I fastened the hinges to the gatepost. This still wasn't the end of the job, since the gate latch was now out of line and wouldn't close. Three screws removed and reset solved the problem and the gate could now be easily opened and securely closed and fastened. By this time the morning was practically gone -- but I didn't forget to clean the clogged drain so my original mission was completed. This is an example of the "simple life" one leads on the farm.

## APRIL (1976)

Things are beginning to grow fast now so I am constantly after weeds, and there are still a few corners that have to be cleaned up. I've pruned the fuchsias and hydrangeas and have fertilized the flower garden and watered the granules into the soil. The greenhouse is getting a long needed going over -- cleaning up the plants and pruning those needing it and repotting many of the plants. It does begin to look better.

The potatoes are hilled and the peas are growing well. The turnips are large enough to be transplanted, and I must get that done soon. I'm waiting for a cool misty day -- weather that is recommended for transplanting. I'm going to plant some beans and squash pretty soon. It may be too early but who can tell this year about the weather. I'll wait a bit for corn and cucumbers. I think it is too early to plant out tomatoes and peppers yet, but cabbages can be set out any time -- and cabbages includes broccoli, cauliflower, kale, etc.

If any one wants a wildcat I have one I'd like to get rid of. He has taken a fancy to chicken in his diet and hangs around hoping for another sample. When and if I let the chickens into the orchard to scratch and forage I have to stay nearby. The dog isn't much help, he doesn't even bark when the cat is around. The boss says to shoot him -- from a distance -- with bird-shot. *If* I can catch him in a trap (humane) we can take him far away and turn him loose.

I wonder if there will be wildflowers this year. So far I see no sign that there will be many anywhere around. The grasses have headed out already in most places. My father used to say that the trees made more than average growth in dry years.

Late last summer I used some "pre-emergence weed control" preparation on some of the garden paths. This stuff is to prevent seeds from germinating, and is supposed to last about two years. It has certainly saved me a lot of work (effort I can put to more profitable use) for the paths have remained clean. This isn't a little effort saved because the main path through the garden is about 150 feet long and 6 feet wide, and there are several other smaller paths. Good stuff; and I see no ill effects on the plants nearby. Of course one could not use it where seeds were to be planted in the future.

## MAY (1978)

The wildflowers are coming out rapidly and abundantly now. Filaree has put a pink frosting on many of the fields and slopes along the road to Salinas. Annual lupine makes blue splashes, while owl's clover, yellow pansies, cream cups, buttercups and California poppies brighten most grassy areas on that road as well as along the coast. Our cars speed along so rapidly that one must watch carefully so as not to miss these flashes of bloom.

I've been helping (?) the boss clean out some of our walking trails and enjoy finding ferns and flowers as we work: brodeias, clematis, fat Solomon seal, white pop-corns, a few early harebells, blue iris, poppies, and the delicate annual snapdragon.

It is time to plant beans, squash, cucumbers, and corn and by the end of the month the tomatoes and peppers should go out into the garden. We are enjoying our first new potatoes. They are a little "cradle-snatched" but they do taste good. In a recent article I read about potatoes, the term "new potatoes" was applied to all recently dug potatoes, as compared to those from storage. In my book, "new potatoes" are immature ones whose skins easily slip off by rubbing; and when cooked these have quite a distinctive flavor and are very tender. Peas are blooming, and so are the strawberries and blackberries. Turnips will soon be large enough to use.

92

The last spring shower (I measured over 5 inches for April 15 and 16th) about finished my lovely ranunculus so I will have to replace them soon. The bulbous iris are beautiful right now -- purple, blue and white ones. The pale blue and the yellow ones bloom earlier and are gone now. The roses are beginning to bloom, as well as many other flowers, so the garden looks bright and gay.

JUNE (1973)

The garden is growing better but still not as well as usual and I still cannot figure why it is so poor this season. However new potatoes and green peas are on the menu and crisp little radishes. Tomatoes are blooming and blackberries ripening. We had quite a lot of strawberries (both wild and garden type). In the orchard there will soon be loquats ripening and early plums. The begonia tubers are ready to be potted or planted out. The roses have been full of flowers, making the garden smell wonderful. When they finish bloom I will clip off all old bloom and fertilize lightly and before long there will be more flowers.

Some time ago someone asked me if I felt that the increase of people in Big Sur -- visitors, campers and residents -- would destroy some species of our native plants. It may; but I am far more concerned about the introduction of other plants, which could crowd out some of the more fragile of our natives. The perennial red peas along the road near Nepenthe and Ventana (these have little fragrance) and the annual white sweetpeas near the Molera Ranch are beautiful as they bloom each year, but some of the plants coming in are not so welcome. A few years ago a few Italian thistles showed up in one of the camping areas here. While this is an annual and not particularly objectionable, it is spreading rapidly and I feel we could well do without it. A few plants are now in bloom beside the highway near Bixby Bridge so it is getting a foothold. The yellow broom is rapidly spreading along the Highway. It is not unattractive while in bloom but it has now reached a point where eradication would be almost impossible. Within the last three years hedge parsley has become prevalent and it is a minor nuisance when its small tenacious burrs get in one's clothing and stockings. I have been trying to keep this little pest out of our orchard, which means going over the area and pulling out all the plants by hand before they bloom and seed. It is rather a losing battle since there is a great deal growing outside the fence.

Some 60 or 70 years ago my father saw the first plant of the milk or Spanish thistle in this area. It grew on the Sur flats where an imported cow had died. Now there are millions of its offspring spread up and down the coast. My mother enjoyed trying new plants in her garden and I can remember Dad saying, "If the cows will eat it, then that plant won't become a bad pest in the country." I think he had a point there.

JULY (1979)

Several people have asked me what they can do for peachleaf curl. That is a fungus disease that makes the leaves on a peach tree curl and distort, the affected leaf is thickened and becomes yellowish or white in color. There is nothing that can be done now, a strong force of water from a nozzled hose will often knock off the affected leaves. The tree usually will put out new leaves and growth. A cold, wet spring is thought to make this disease worse. To control peachleaf curl a "dormant spray," lime-sulphur, or Bordeaux mixture should be used in late fall or winter and again just as the buds begin to swell, a third spraying as the buds show pink color is recommended by some. I *try* to follow this schedule and it certainly helps. I had to spray several extra times this spring since the growth did not all start at the same time, and even so there were a few deformed leaves on some of the trees. If only a few leaves are affected, little harm is done, but if most of the leaves show the curl (fruit and twigs can be affected also), then the tree will be weakened.

The freezing-canning schedule has started for me. Green peas are frozen, and blackberries are ripening for jelly, jam and juice.

The "sugar snap" peas proved very successful. The vines are now 7-1/2 to 8 feet tall and I need something to stand on to reach the top pods. This is a new type of "snow pea" with edible pods and can be used while the pods are still flat and also when the peas are well formed and the pods are plump. They are very tender and sweet, and the sweetness seems to increase as the pods get plumper. I think this is a really valuable addition to the vegetable garden. I have frozen some and will plant a new crop before long for winter vegetable. Work is being done to develop a dwarf growing sugar snap pea.

The summer vegetables (beans, cucumbers, peppers, tomatoes, zucchini, etc.) are growing -- but slowly so far. Shall I blame the weather, or my lateness in getting them started?

We have had a doe and her two spotted babies coming each late afternoon to nibble vetch that grows outside our large window. They are interesting to watch, but mama is easily alarmed and then they all go bouncing away. Most of this spring we have had very few birds using the feed and water station. Recently quite a variety of birds have been coming, and there are two young hummingbirds now fighting with each other and the parents as to who shall control their juice bar. And I spent most of a half hour trying to catch or shoo out one of the young ones that was in the greenhouse. I had a butterfly net on a long handle but couldn't swing it efficiently for fear of breaking glass; so around and around we went until the poor little thing was almost worn out -- and me too!

## AUGUST (1968)

It seems that my life recently has been one canned thing after another. Apricots are canned and jammed (both cooked jam and frozen). Blackberries have been made into juice and jam. A few pies are stored in the freezer -- both of berries and apricots. The beets are all pickled and in glass jars. I canned a few loquats and even bought a few cherries and canned them. I have started freezing string beans for winter too. Next I'll make some green applesauce and can that for future reference. I'm not really grieving that we won't have a surplus of peaches this year, but I will probably can a few jars when they ripen faster than we can eat them. I will can pears later and tomatoes, but the shelves are beginning to fill up with full jars.

Since the blackberries are through bearing for this year and I had a little remodeling to do on the trellis, I did the main pruning of our berries. This is an excellent time to prune out the vines that produced fruit this spring (they will die back anyway soon) and remove all new shoots except 4 or 5 of the strongest. These reserved shoots should be tied up to the trellis and will produce next year's crop.

I have planted seed of cabbage, cauliflower, broccoli, etc., for winter vegetables. And will soon plant more beans, squash, and corn for late fall. Tomatoes are setting well and peppers are blooming but neither are ready to use.

In the flower department -- begonias and fuchsias are looking pretty good, they get a regular feeding every two weeks. Roses are giving a few flowers, and the mums are growing tall in spite of being cut back last month. I have a big job waiting me -- that is to dig up a lot of my daffodils which are much too thick after being left in the ground about 4 years. When the bulbs are out I'll dig a wide trench, put bone meal generously in the bottom, then 2 inches of soil and set the bulbs on that soil, covering them with about 3 inches of soil.

I find everything needs extra thorough watering this summer, due to low rainfall last winter.

I have to show my foot to that fresh rooster every once in a while -- just to refresh his memory.

## SEPTEMBER (1977)

Whew! I'm glad all that fire is past. We can still smell the smoke and will continue to do so until we have a rain to thoroughly cleanse the air. It is tragic that this should have happened but I think many persons are glad that all that tinder-dry fuel is gone from the back country and that there are now some good fire-roads around and into this large wilderness area. Those spectacular and huge mushrooms of smoke that arose over the mountains in the early part of the fire looked like atomic bomb explosions, and someone estimated that the energy generated when a thousand acres went up in flames was equal to that of an atomic bomb. Some days we would see as many as a dozen of these. I'm glad that the community is preparing for what may happen when the rains come. After the example of 1972 of what can occur with intense downpour -- even for a short period -- people are conscious of the potential danger from the river when some 90 percent of the watershed has been denuded. No one can predict what may happen.

I haven't been doing so much in the garden except to keep things watered. We had plenty of uninvited guests at the late ripening apricot tree. I caught 1 coon and 3 foxes and there were blue jays in abundance. There is still a coon (I think) that has been sampling the few peaches that are beginning to ripen. It is a constant struggle to get *part* of the fruit that is on the trees. Dwarf trees in a wire cage might be the answer. The vegetables aren't doing as well as some years. But we have more than we can use -- string beans, green corn, zucchini, peppers, cucumbers and a few tomatoes are now beginning to ripen. There are plenty of flowers in bloom and I need to spend some time planting out late blooming things to keep the garden bright. If you do it soon, the winter vegetables can be planted now -- cabbage types as well as carrots, lettuce, turnips, mustard, radishes, etc. Peas planted now will usually produce a good crop. I usually plant the edible podded peas at this time for use as a winter vegetable.

Not long ago the boss took me with him up into the higher part of Juan Higuera Creek that was so fire and flood damaged in 1972. The creek was running well in spite of our drought. The flood changed the area somewhat. It is far more open now due to trees having been burned -- some fallen by the flood. Lots of seedling trees are starting in the gravel and rocks beside the stream -- redwoods, maples and many madrones. I was amazed at the quantities of scarlet mimulus growing along the creek, making it bright with its brilliant flowers. This is a plant more rare than common in our area and I was delighted to see such an abundant growth of it. I haven't seen it in upper Phenegar Creek. There were a lot of five-finger ferns well started also. It was a nice little excursion and a pleasure to see the streamside healing over so well.

OCTOBER (1974)

For us this is the year of the rodents. In early summer we were bothered by tree squirrels after the fruit in the orchard. And now we have field mice. They lived and multiplied in the grass which grew after the seeding followed the fire. Now that they have eaten all the grass and seed they are seeking more food. They started chewing on the trunks of the fruit trees, especially the young trees and citrus. So I cleared all the vegetation and leaves well away from all the trees, thus removing all mouse shelter, and painted the trunks with repellent. Recently these little pests have moved into the flower and vegetable garden and I'm trying to trap them. One afternoon, in broad daylight, they cut off and carried away 48 just ready-to-bloom marigold plants from the bed where I had recently transplanted them! I found all the plant tops, *uneaten* piled behind a small rock wall. I have 4 plants left in that bed beside a few of the eaten off ones that are making some new growth. The important thing is that I caught 2 field mice that did all that damage. Woodrats are determined to set up housekeeping in the chicken house. Also caught a ground squirrel there. Chipmunks are busy eating the grapes on the lathhouse, before they are ripe enough to pick. And mice (at least that is all I catch in the trap that I set up in the tree crotch) climb up into the avocado tree and nibble on ripening fruits. Sometimes I find a partially eaten avocado on the ground in the morning -- more often just the seed. Takes awhile each evening to set the traps and in the morning to check them all.

## NOVEMBER (1968)

The boss took the honey from the bees and we extracted it. We decided that the bees had gathered much nectar from the cascara for some of the honey had quite a bitter flavor. That can be used for feeding the bees during the winter or early spring when they need building up. I have been busy getting the long-legged roosters ready for the freezer. And as though that were not enough, we got 5 young ducks which we will fatten and also tuck into that freezer.

I've been picking apples and pears and gathering the fallen walnuts before the coyote discovers that they are almost as nourishing as the avocados which he samples every night. I get those that fall during daytime.

That was a fine little rain we had but not enough to last long -- so we keep watering. The wild grass seed has started growing out on the hill and more rain will be needed soon to keep it from drying out. Where some old grass was left to protect the little plants, they can survive quite a while but where the area has been too closely pastured, there may be some loss. We'll hope more seed is still in the ground to sprout and grow later.

These summery days are doing well to ripen the tomatoes and the late figs, and we are enjoying both. I make a round of the orchard starting with a fig or two picked at just the correct stage of ripeness, then a sample of the well ripened Concord grapes, maybe a Seckle pear or a crisp Golden Delicious apple right off the tree and finish off with a still undried walnut so sweet when the thin skin is removed from the kernel. Who needs much of a regulation meal after all that?

## DECEMBER (1968)

Mr. Coyote and I have just about solved the unemployment problem. He insists on visiting the orchard and digs a hole under the fence at night; I fill these up next day with old fence wire, rocks, boards, broken glass, brush or whatever I think will stop him. Next night he digs another hole and I fill it up, etc. etc. etc.! The boss says I can't keep him out, and I say I can be as persistent as a coyote. I suppose when the coyote is living on a few toyon berries, some grasshoppers or beetles, an occasional mouse or mole (even the best coyote doesn't get a wild pig very often) then a couple of small avocados, a walnut or so and windfall apple or pear might be ample incentive to dig under the fence and into the orchard for an extra snack. I don't mind the fruit he eats but when he gets to feeling right at home, he'll come around during daytime and could help himself to a nice fat hen or two.

I've been cleaning up the garden -- old plants, leaves, weeds, etc. By doing this now there are fewer hiding places for bugs during winter and hopefully there will be fewer pests come spring.

So have a Merry Christmas -- remember the story of the woman who was disappointed in her husband's gift to her -- he had given her a diamond necklace and she wanted a load of fertilizer for her garden.

Esther Pfeiffer Ewoldsen

from THE ROUND-UP

Selected by Beverly Ewoldsen

*Mr. and Mrs. Ernest Carving -- 6 ft. and 5 ft. 2 in., wood*

*Mrs. E. Carving is out of one piece of redwood, her sweater the bark, her skirt the sapwood and her face and hands the interior.*

*Mr. Ernest Carving is a piece of cedar for the legs, stained ash, redwood sawdust and resin for the sweater and Alaska cedar for the shirt. Redwood face and hands. In both cases I started with the shoes first and worked up.*

*"Big Sur is not a peaceful environment to me... everything fights you... you can't tame it, and for that, one should be grateful." So states Barbara Spring, successful sculptor, wife and mother.*

# An Interview with Barbara Spring

## by Kristin Trotter

When I arrived at the Burns Creek home of Bill and Barbara Spring, I found Barbara in her workshop bent over the headless body of a neatly dressed old woman holding a handbag.

"Poor Miss Woods," said Barbara, giving her sculpture a little pat. "She's had a nasty fall."

Outside the workshop a pair of legs stood upside down, tennis shoes in the air. "Do you think it will rain," Barbara said, glancing up at the darkening sky, "or can we leave these legs outside while we have a cup of tea?"

In the house, Barbara busied herself putting the kettle on and stoking up the fire while I wandered around, not quite sure what was real and what was not. A cello player peeks out from the upstairs loft, a shelf of wooden books holds a tray of wooden hors d'oeuvres, hooks are hung with wooden frying pans and wooden cuts of meat. A giant set of wooden car keys hangs above the door.

"Well, all right," said Barbara, settling down beside the fire. "What do you want to know?"

I was born in Essex, England, but I was raised on the coast of Wales -- a very wild place, similar to Big Sur. When I was ten my father died and we moved to Kent. Again it was a very wild place out in the country. My mother started a poultry farm. We had no electricity, no car or anything. I went to school at Charles Dickens' home, Gads Hill Place, which had been made into a girls' school -- then Gravesend School of Art and finally to Central School of Art in London. I started as a painter, but one day I found a hunk of clay -- actual clay out of the ground, and I started working with it, making shapes and

I soon switched my studies to sculpture.

When World War II broke out I joined the WAAFS and that's how I met Bill. I was in the Air Force on Radar and he was in that cloak and dagger thing -- what do you call it? -- the OSS. I had to do plotting of our bombers going out to fight the Germans. I went to Art School in the evenings sometimes walking five miles back home in the blackout. In a way it was very exciting. Later Bill and I were married and after the children were born I gave up art -- didn't touch it again for about ten years. The night Cynthia was born there was an air raid that knocked out part of the house. Frances was born next, and she was early because the goat butted me. Goat induction, you might call it.

When the war was over we moved to Long Island, and then to Rochester where we lived in an old abandoned farm house on the banks of Lake Ontario for $25.00 a month. The kids must have been about 6 and 7 then. The inside was so filthy that we had to cook outside over a campfire. Cynthia fell into the fire once, and had a terrible scar for years. Then Frances got her leg run over by a tractor. We were so hard up that I hired out to pick fruit taking the girls with me. We were picking cherries when Frances fell off the ladder right in front of the tractor. She was all right, thank God, but what we went through!

One morning Bill came in and he was shaving and he said to me, "How would you like to go to California?" I don't know what brought that on, but I said, "When do we leave?" We crossed the country in an ancient Oldsmobile and the kids had their feet hanging out the windows because it was so hot. When we got to California we had no job, no house, no nothing. We stayed in a hotel, then a trailer, then in a boarding house. Finally we put an ad in the paper and somebody called and offered us a house in San Francisco. She is still our friend today. I got a job teaching art in a private school in Pacific Heights and Bill got the Hi Fi Shop. Our next door neighbor was Charlie Levitsky's sister and it was through Charlie that we started coming down to Big Sur and rented the old hospital building at Anderson Canyon for $12.50 a month. This was the building where the Chinese laborers were treated during the time the road was being made -- around the early thirties I think. We spent all our holidays there. It turned out that I already had connections with people in Big Sur. I didn't meet Eric Barker until we came here, but I had known his wife Madeline Green for years through a folk dance group in San Francisco. Then there was Varda -- I had taught his child Vagadu in art school.

Eventually we lost that house because the land was sold, but by that time we'd met Boris and Filippa Veren and when they went to France we bought that house at Burns Creek and moved here permanently.

I was a full-time sculptor by then -- well, I guess I had been full-time since 1958 when I gave up teaching and started wood carving. I was doing vegetation -- cactus and organic stuff, probably inspired by Melissa (Blake) Levitsky's garden. She had a tremendous garden -- all kinds of cacti and rare plants. When we moved here my work changed from vegetation to people in trapped situations.

*Photo by K.E. Ohm*

*Barbara Spring*

*Annabelle's Aunt -- 3 ft., wood*

In 1962 I had my first one man show with Marcelle Labaudt, one of the oldest galleries in San Francisco. I say one man show and not one woman show because of my age. I'm 65 and nobody said one woman show back then, but I don't think of myself as a man or a woman or anything else when I work. It doesn't make a damn bit of difference what I am -- I am a sculptor. But then of course it really *does* make a difference and my work reflects it. I have a terrible time with men in my sculpture. In several of my scenes I do away with them altogether. There is the one with the woman and her cats, and the man has disappeared. "Willy's Mother" is its title. I never intended to do her at all, and certainly not the way she is. I wanted to do Willy, and then decided to give him a mother later, and I also gave his mother some cats. Filippa came over one day and she said she knew a woman who had 40 cats, and I thought, perfect! I'll make Willy's mother totally involved in her cats.

I've carved 20 cats and I'm exhausted! There was no father in the scene, but eventually I put in a portrait of him in wood. He has no chin...you see I have a nasty side to me! I have no control over it, and I don't try to stop it. I am not anti-male since, like Georgia O'Keeffe, most of my help has come from them -- both my husband Bill and my gallery, William Sawyer, have supported me during times when I sold nothing and they did not question what I was doing. That also goes for the males who for years have so generously supplied me with wood and physical help.

I have the best source of wood here in Big Sur that I've ever had, but it is not a peaceful environment to me at all. It's a fighting environment, not like England or Wales where you feel the peace of centuries and centuries of people tilling the soil. It's the most hostile place I've ever lived. Oh, not the people, of course, they are the *least* hostile, but the land just can't be tamed -- everything fights you -- and for that we should be thankful. A lot of artists come to Big Sur with the intention of painting but the environment is so powerful that they can't do it, so they sit around drinking and goofing off all day. I work 6 hours a day not looking at the landscape. If you look at the landscape, you're done for.

I'm very interested in how powerful women are in the world today. I don't think we necessarily want to be. I used to stir Bill's tea, put the sugar in, do everything for him and the girls until they were teenagers, but when I became a full-time sculptor I gradually had to wean every one of those things away from me, and the three of them in return became my most realistic critics. It's difficult to have a family and a profession. Here again it goes back to my mother. She was the meekest little thing until my father died and then she became a very powerful woman. We *had* to do a man's work on the farm, so the chain saws and chisels that I work with in my profession are perfectly natural to me.

You see, we are what we are because of what we've come through. That's what I'm trying to show in my sculpture environments. Willy's mother is the way she is because of what has happened in her life, just like the rest of us.

*Photos by Richard Sargent*

*Willy's Mother*

There is a sudden gust of wind and then the sound of raindrops. Barbara jumps up, "My God, there's the rain. I'll have to go and bring those legs in."

As I leave the Spring's house and start over Burns Creek I catch sight of another one of Barbara's sculptures which has become a local landmark. The Meditator sits cross-legged beside the pool, day and night, watching over the canyon. I remember a time when Bill Spring and I, working together at the Coast Gallery, were asked by a tour bus driver, "Hey, do either of you know who that guru guy is down there at Burns Creek? The guy must be really dedicated because he's out there meditating every time I drive by."

Bill chuckled and gave me a wink. "That's a friend of my wife's," he told the driver. "He's taking a course at Esalen."

*Old age in Big Sur can be hard -- especially for an active woman like Lulu May Harlan who spent most of her 92 years doing both a man's and a woman's work.*

# Old Age in Big Sur: Lulu Harlan

*by Kathleen O'Shaughnessy*

I met and talked to Lulu May Harlan only three times and yet so firmly imprinted was this lady upon my mind after our first meeting that when I was asked to write about her for this book, I knew the rightness of it.

Our first contact came on a warm, late summer afternoon when my friend, Katy, said, "Let's go pick apples at the Harlan Ranch." I had some vague impression that the name Harlan was associated with the Lucia Lodge along the southern coast of the Big Sur mountain range, but that was all. Always open to new explorations in Big Sur, I said, "Sure, let's go. We can make applesauce out of them at my place tonight."

By the time we reached the final gate, which opened in a special way to fool the Harlan's clever goats, I was already in love with the place. Lulu's youngest brother, Marion, (who died in 1983) met us, and while he and Katy exchanged stories and brought each other up to date about life since their last meeting, I immersed myself in what was around me.

The grapes were not quite ripe yet, but their healthy vines spread themselves on a light hillside to the right of twin barns built some 50 years ago by Marion himself. I was told one barn housed box after box of canned applesauce. Its twin barn housed a magnificent collection of tools -- old ones -- the kind that still had fine steel in them and were dependable and indestructable.

There was a pile of chopped wood near Marion's cabin, stacked with precision. We moved toward the orchard then and began filling our bellies at about the same rate we were filling our boxes.

The sun was moving along and Marion's goats needed attention, so Katy volunteered that we would "see to Lulu."

We moved then between the orchard and Lulu's old cabin. The weeds were high, the fence was rickety, the tree to the left of the gate was in need of pruning. A huge pink rose hung so near the gate that we had to side-step it. The sun's separated rays filtered through the redwoods growing out of the canyon to the right of the cabin.

It was cold now that there was no longer direct sunlight and I felt relief to step from Lulu's small wooden porch into her living room and find a fire going in her small woodstove.

The room had a long-ago and familiar quality to it -- it was lived in and cared about. Pictures of Lulu's family -- original homesteaders in these primeval mountains -- were in abundance. I peeped into the room between the living room and kitchen and saw many jars of home-canned goods and a partially folded wheelchair.

Lulu herself sat with her legs close to the stove. She could not move well for her joints, particularly in her legs, were arthritic. Her face became lighter as she recognized Katy. She shook hands politely with me and Katy began quizzing her about how she felt and about recent events.

Soon she was feeling tired and we offered to "do whatever needed doing" to prepare her for bed and a comfortable night.

"Can you reach your walker from here?"

"Put my slippers near the bed and towards the foot, so I can slip my feet right into them."

We arranged the sheets so they would not tangle her in the night and keep her from being able to get up. When all seemed to be in place, she asked that we leave the kitchen door open as we left, but to close the screen door.

As Katy and I moved along the narrow hallway and towards the kitchen door, I heard Lulu say softly to herself in a manner that indicated that it was a nightly ritual, "I hope the Lord decides to take me tonight."

She was 92 years old and she was ready to go.

* * *

Lulu May Harlan was born January 9, 1892, the eldest child of Wilbur Judson Harlan and Ada Amanda Dani, at Lucia Ranch, "beyond the redwood grove," where she lived her entire life until she was taken to a nursing home in Monterey not long after the above meeting in the Fall of 1982.

Her father had homesteaded the land and the original 167 acre claim was filed in San Francisco in 1885. He married in Santa Cruz on July 7, 1889. His family grew and grew, so after the tenth child he built a large, two story, white and red-roofed house with timbers cut from a sawmill powered by a waterwheel he had built after digging a ditch between the Dani and Harlan creeks to supply the water. The new home was spacious enough to house his large family plus a schoolteacher. Two of the Harlan sons subsequently married two of the school-teachers.

"Aunt Lu" did both a man's and a woman's work on the ranch. She was the postmistress of Lucia beginning in 1938, held potluck dinners for the family every Father's Day, and ran Lucia Lodge between 1964 and 1970.

*Lucia Lodge opened after the high-way was built in 1935, I think. I didn't work the Lodge right away. My father leased it out to a man and his wife before I took it. I was already in my sixties and had been in an auto wreck in Salinas. I was*

104

laid up in a big cast and was on crutches. The good leg got stiff because I used it so much and I couldn't get around very well for eight months. I was too old, had to use a cane to get around with. I said I would run the Lodge for at least five years. I thought I would last that long. But I ran it six and then a nephew, John, came with his wife and said they would like to run it. It was a good chance to keep it in the family. They ran it ten years and now their boys have taken it over.

In an interview with Lulu in 1982, she spoke of many day-to-day things which made up life in the Santa Lucia Mountains, everything from dogs to food preservation to courting along the southern coast during her youth.

*I wasn't much stuck on boys. My brother Marion has taken care of me and we are the only two in the family who didn't get married.*

*We had dances -- I can't remember if it was once a week or once a month now. We had picnics in various spots around. Everybody dressed up and it was fun. I didn't like dancing, but I liked the music that they had, so I used to go once in awhile and listen, but when you live on a ranch there is something to do practically all the time, so I didn't go much.*

*We always had a dog. With more than one they would always be into mischief -- chasing deer or running away from home. A man beyond the redwoods had two dogs. They came up here and attacked Marion's goats. Marion shot one dog and killed it. The vet said about the second dog, "Looks like a mountain lion mauled this dog."*

Lulu said she had never been afraid as a little girl. "Some people scare their children, but not us."

*Father spanked us often as children. I can't remember what for. I guess that made good children out of us.*

Courtesy of Ruth and John Harlan

*Us kids got along well except for one brother who was a tormenter to everyone. Then he got to be sociable.*

*We learned right from the start by working with our parents. We would milk our half of the cows, learned how to plant potatoes, corn, wheat, beans -- everything. We had a wonderful life. Both the girls and the boys learned indoor and outdoor work. Father held Sunday School and read the Bible to us. There was a small organ (still a keepsake in Lulu's cabin). There were 20 children in school. It was hard for me to make R's. I would sit on the bedroom floor and I would make R's until I could make them good.*

*I was used to being alone after my father passed away. My mother had a heart attack and died suddenly. My father lingered on and I took care of him -- giving him the bed pan and sponge baths for two solid weeks. I was just about wore out, but I lasted. I took good care of both of them. I cut down then and didn't have chickens or so many cows so I wouldn't have to work so hard.*

Since Lulu was famous for her good food, we asked about that. Of course they had canned and baked bread and cured meat. It was necessary to this way of life.

*My father had bees and we made honey candy. We boiled the honey down, let it cool, and then we would pull on it until it was a nice amber color. Then we'd cut it with a scissors from a big long string, like taffy. Mother made candy from sugar, but we liked the honey candy.*

*I never drank soda pop enough to know what it was like. When I tasted wine, I thought it was horrible stuff and I didn't see how anybody could like it. I weighed 260 and had a heart attack while I was working at the Lodge. They took me to the hospital and the doctor said not to drink pop or eat spices and sugar. I went down to 160. A lady used to cook for me and dole out the food, so I lost gradually. As long as I went to the doctor my pulse and blood pressure weren't too high. I thought there was no use going to him because everything was the same for so many years. I liked to take skin treatments because my skin would get scabs and raw places and knobs grew on my elbows. The skin doctor would take them off for me, but now I'm not able to go.*

*We weren't sick much because we were fed good and we were isolated. When you don't mix with people, you don't catch things. I had a girl here to take care of me, but Marion and I kept catching things that she brought here and all she was interested in was the money. She finally got a job in Pebble Beach.*

*I can't wait on myself anymore. My brother helps with most of it. I can't manipulate my body. But this morning I creamed my own mush before my brother got here and got up and dressed myself. I enjoyed hard work all my life, but now I'm ready to go and I don't know why the Good Lord don't take me. I'm not enjoying life so good because I'm so lame.*

Lulu Harlan took a bad fall in the autumn of 1982 and was found on the floor by her attentive brother Marion. She had been falling down a lot, but this time it was bad, and now a decision had to be made about caring for her before she broke a bone. She was taken to a nursing home in Pacific Grove at age 91.

* * *

On January 7th, I had on my town list "Visit Lulu at Nursing Home." It was hot and windy as I stepped through the door of the nursing facility, through a long hallway filled with wheelchairs and elderly people milling about.

I found my way to Lulu's doorway. She was sleeping in a wheelchair with her small face turned sideways on her bedside table, taking a nap. She looked so doll-like and alone. I gently touched her hand and said her name.

We had a good visit. I massaged her hands and arms with sweet smelling lotion and we told Big Sur and Lucia mountain stories to each other until I saw she was tired. I helped her into bed, arranging the covers the way she liked them and promised ice cream on my next town trip.

"What kind do you like?" I asked and she said "Oh, all kinds."

\* \* \*

Soon came the Coast storms of 1983, savage and isolating and taxing to the psyche and body. On Good Friday in April of 1983 Lulu's baby brother Marion succumbed to flu, heart attack, and stress. I knew I would not feel complete with Lulu until I went to see her again.

It was not until the road opened to the north that once again I entered into the surrealistic world of Lulu's nursing home, clutching peach ice cream in a paper bag with my heart skipping. How would I find Lulu now that she had been given the terrible news of her beloved brother's death?

She was sitting in her wheelchair beside her bed -- this time sitting straight and watching me approach. She had what looked like a brand new hair trim and her eyes were very clear.

I dished up ice cream and she waved off an offer to help her with the spoon. Her fingers seemed a little more flexible and sure than I had remembered them.

I traded her up-to-date stories about Big Sur for old stories about Big Sur, sitting close so she could hear me and so I could read her face. She told me Marion had been cremated and his ashes taken to his treasured "Tank House," just as he had requested. Only once did a sad cloud flash across her face. How I loved her iron strength.

\* \* \*

Lulu Harlan died on May 22, 1984, the last of the original pioneer women of the Big Sur coast.

*Based on an interview with Lulu Harlan by Charlotte Redstone*

# Esalen Women

*by Joyce Rogers Lyke*

# Afterword

*Today, February 22, 1985, as this book that I dreamed of ten years ago stands poised on the printer's doorstep, I end as I began in the Foreword, on a personal note.*

*The process of creation has sustained me in a decade the keynote of which has been CHANGE. Throughout three years of drought, a major forest fire, an earthquake or two, not to mention the 18 month demise of Highway One, and a personal life that seemed to mimic nature, devotion to the craft of writing has been a means to deal with my experience. Six small self-published books later, I believe that the process of creating has given me the focus that has enabled me to stay in paradise. Without "my work," I would never have made it this far.*

*Of these books, the seventh, BIG SUR WOMEN, has most nourished me. Contacts with wonderful women—both those I have met in the flesh, as well as those on tape, in type, and in the spirit— have filled a vital need for confirmation and companionship. These women, scattered in time and living far apart, have been my support group, my foundation. I have learned from each many diverse ways to adapt to the demands of life in this wilderness.*

*Have I found the balance that I seek—a way for a woman to live a satisfying life here? I regret to report that there is no formula, no clear-cut solution. It appears, for me at least, that the search for balance is a constant, a perpetual tightrope walk necessitating constant subtle adjustments, having little or nothing to do with where I live or with my life style, but only with who I am. Perhaps this is true of all of us.*

*To live in Big Sur is no panacea; nevertheless, I can't think of anyplace else in the world I would rather be. I still live alone in a cabin on a mountainside; I caretake, I garden, I walk. Those days when I don't find the time for a walk are like days without love.*

*I know that in order to stay in this paradise, I must be satisfied with what is here. I must love my life. Unless I can stay flexible and willing to accommodate to its demands, the coast will sluff me off, as it has so many others, like so much crumbling earth. I know that I am only passing through this place, and that my years in Big Sur have been the highpoint and the greatest love of my life.*

In the production and design of BIG SUR WOMEN, I have not been alone. Pat Addleman has taken the raw manuscript and seen it through the maze of modern technology onto the printed page. For her artist's eyes, for her firm support, I am grateful.

I also want to thank these women whose contributions have greatly enriched my understanding of what it means to be a Big Sur woman: Ruth Albee, Kathy Blyth, Norma Bohrer, Theodora Sue Crowley, Tara Evans, Arwyn Evenstar, Beverly Ewoldsen, Esther Ewoldsen, Lulu May Harlan, Sally Hawkins, Elfrieda Hayes, Heidi Hopkins, Nancy Hopkins, Susan Hubbard, Deborah Johansen, Melissa Blake Levitsky, Jaki Lewis, Nancy Mayer, Deborah Medow, Rosa Nash, Kathleen O'Shaughnessy, Marvel Philips, Charlotte Redstone, Celia Sanborn, Nancy Sanders, Barbara Spring, Kate Stromberger, Virginia Swanson, Cindy Summers, Holly Thauwald, Kristin Trotter, Eby Wold.